the
peacemakers

By Ella May Miller

The Joy of Housekeeping
I Am a Mother
The Peacemakers

Ella May Miller

the peacemakers

How to find peace and share it

Fleming H. Revell Company
Old Tappan, New Jersey

Library of Congress Cataloging in Publication Data

Miller, Ella May.
    The peacemakers.

    1. Peace (Theology) 2. Christian life—Mennonite authors. I. Title.
BT736.4.M5   248'.48'97   77–1625
ISBN 0–8007–0865–2

The Peacemakers

Introduction

People are peacemakers.

No armies or battlegrounds or legislatures can make peace. Only persons can do that as they dedicate their intellect and reason to the issue at hand and work at resolving the conflict. Persons make a treaty.

Usually we think of the peacemaker as the negotiator between two warring nations, between two factions, between the employer and employee—the one who signs a treaty. In a sense he is a peacemaker.

But there's another kind of peacemaker I think is very important. It's the person who lives in such a way as to avoid wars and strikes, strife and hostilities.

Peacemakers are people thus dedicated to peacemaking. They commit their minds, their bodies, their desires—their total selves—to God's control. They become servants to those around them. They meet the needs of others out of a caring, compassionate heart—a heart full of God's love.

Peacemakers are persons in everyday living—loving, caring, and sharing in the home, community, shops, schools, offices, everyplace.

Because of a woman's deep and lasting influence on those she relates to, beginning in the home, I dedicate this book to her as I write from a woman's perspective. However, I recognize that every person, man or woman, will be able to identify with much of the book.

I've based my chapters on the following appropriate and wise Chinese proverb which, incidentally, intrigues me very much:

The Way to Peace

If there is righteousness in the heart,
　　There will be beauty in the character.
If there is beauty in the character,
　　There will be harmony in the home.
If there is harmony in the home,
　　There will be order in the nation.
If there is order in the nation,
　　There will be peace in the world.

"Blessed are the peacemakers, for they shall be called the sons of God."

Matthew 5:9 RSV

1
Peace . . . Peace

Is there peace on earth?

As I write this chapter, nations are suspicious of each other, some actively engaged in warfare. Others display a surface peace while at the same time competing among themselves to be or to remain country number one.

There wasn't any peace at an airport recently when a bomb concealed in a locker exploded, killing ten people and injuring others.

Nor is there peace in the home in a nearby community. Just recently the wife related how she initiated divorce proceedings a year ago. Then her husband suggested a week of vacation together—just the two of them—in an effort to resolve their conflicts. They're still together. Things seem much better. However, she confessed, "Lately I don't talk to him at all. I don't come to him for anything. He said, 'I won't fight. I'll do all I can to stay together. I love you and the children.' "

Strikes flare up by teachers, doctors, day laborers. Riots rock schools, prison camps, and communities.

In many countries there are wars. We ourselves are not engaged in civil or international wars, but political wars, economic wars, intellectual, social, and spiritual wars exist.

How does all this square up with the angel's message nearly two thousand years ago to those lowly shepherds on the Judean hills? He announced the birth of a Savior, and "Peace upon earth among men of goodwill."

I cringe at the news of fighting and wars—be it on an international, national, state, community, or home level. I, for one, often cry, "Lord, when will this peace come? All this slaughter, wounding, suffering, torture, hate, and revenge. All the innocent caught in these wars. God, can't there be peace?"

Then I recall the words of the Savior: ". . . my peace I give to you; not as the world gives do I give to you" (John 14:27 RSV).

A revelation—"not as the world." Ah—the world says that peace is the absence of conflict. It is a friendly condition between two countries, two groups, or two persons. Jesus says, "My peace is different. You can have it even living in the midst of conflict."

You want peace. I want peace—not merely the treaty to end conflict between two warring countries, not merely the interval between two wars, not merely a pact or an agreement to end hostilities between two dissenting groups. We want peace which is the ability to live together harmoniously in spite of differences.

Peace isn't a natural characteristic of persons; therefore it is not natural for governments or nations. Ideas clash. Desires conflict. Goals create tensions. Words produce battles. Passions blaze into fights. No, peace is not a "natural." In order to have peace in society, some individual or group must make peace between conflicting persons and groups and then help maintain peace. So we have peacemakers.

Who are these peacemakers?

Only Jesus can give peace to the individual who experiences the inevitables of life: hurts, misunderstandings, personality clashes, opposing theories and desires. There's peace because you and I love each other. We refuse to hate and hurt each other, to lie and to deceive each other. We trust each other. We have faith in each other.

Peacemakers are persons—not institutions or armies.

2
Who Are the Peacemakers?

Who are the peacemakers? What is their role? Convincing one side to surrender? Resolving conflicts?

The role of peacemaker includes these roles and more. Probably the most important role which we so often overlook is the preventative role. This is living in harmony with others and thereby avoiding conflicts and wars.

Peacemakers are blessed—content and happy, according to the Holy Scriptures. They are called the sons and daughters of God.

Indeed, statesmen who have negotiated treaties are respected and highly honored. We admire the peacemakers who settle industrial strikes and civilian riots. The caliber of persons needed to bring two opposing forces together is one we appreciate. Theirs is a noble task.

Such persons, however, have had to be acquainted with the ways of peace. They are persons who know how to give and take, how to compromise in order to settle differences. According to Dr. Ernest A. Fitzgerald, in *Pace* magazine, they are persons who are "at peace with life . . . those who have gone the 'second mile,' who have done a bit more than was expected."

On a national and international level, these persons are few. But I propose that somewhere they learned the ways of peace. I also propose that you and I, the common persons, are each called to play this much-needed role—that of peacemakers.

Really, that's what this book is all about—exploring ways to maintain peace on a personal, family, and community level; both by living in a way to avoid conflicts and strifes, and by arriving at peaceful solutions when there are conflicts.

Peacemaking hinges on personal relationships, on

thoughts, on words, on deeds, on goals, and on wishes in everyday living.

None of us can pass the buck. It begins within the individual. To live peaceably implies that one lives at peace with self. And the root of personal peace is peace between the individual and his/her Creator, God. It permeates the daily human relationships within the home. Those who live in an atmosphere of peacemaking carry it outside the home into every area of their daily living.

Peacemaking begins at home—with Mom's and Dad's relationships with each other and with their sons and daughters. Dr. Karl Menninger, the famed psychiatrist, claims that we learn to resolve hostility in the home, or we don't learn it at all.

Parents learn the art of peacemaking not by silence—not by accusation—not by "wielding a stick"—but rather by learning to communicate, to share, to give and take.

Children growing up in such an atmosphere learn this art of peacemaking as they observe and absorb Mom's and Dad's examples. They soon infiltrate society as community leaders, department heads, teachers, officers, mayors, statesmen, senators, lawmakers, pastors, and professional persons. They are in a very real sense peacemakers—not only settling controversies but also living in a constructive, positive way which helps to eliminate strife and fights and wars.

I also believe that we mothers basically hold in our hands the key to peaceful family living in the midst of daily struggles, problems, and difficult situations. We, by virtue of our closeness in the child's early, impressionable years, greatly influence his behavior and thought patterns for life. We are the instillers of values, of morals, of goals in our children's lives. Will he live a life of bitterness and hostility? Will he grow up to hate others—minority groups and those who are different from him? Or will he grow up to love and care and share with any and all persons he contacts in his life because we live peaceably and peacefully?

All Christians are involved—mothers, fathers, sons, daughters, relatives, friends, and neighbors. We who love our dear Lord are peacemakers. Every one of us.

Part 1

RIGHTNESS IN THE HEART

"If there is righteousness in the heart,
There will be beauty in the character."

3
Self-understanding

In Argentina, during the week-long celebration of Carnival, young and old disguise themselves in festive costumes. Faces and figures are masked. It is impossible to identify individuals other than your intimate friends. No doubt this originated as a gay festivity. But it has deteriorated into a week of unreality. Not only do the participants disguise their appearance but also their actions. In the disguise of Carnival they allow anything!

We may not go around in costumes of disguise as these folks do, but too many of us go around with masks on our personalities, on our true selves. We lack self-knowledge.

To be right in one's heart demands self-understanding. No one can be at peace with self unless he/she understands self.

Who am I? That's the great question each of us has had to solve somewhere along life's way. Those who haven't solved it are unhappy and are fighting self and others.

A male must understand who he is as uniquely created by God. This is also true for a female.

No woman can enjoy life unless she understands herself as a female—created by God as unique from male, created in His image as a complement to the male. The two, male and female, complete what lacks in each other. The two together—living and working side by side—contribute wholeness to society, both in marriage and out of marriage.

She understands the contribution of her unique glands,

chemistry, and body to personhood. She understands the
endocrinological change that brings in the possible child-
bearing years, then ushers them out again some thirty or
more years later.

She understands the potential placed within her by her
Creator for deep feelings of life—both of joys and of sorrows, of love and of bitterness. As she understands herself,
she can place her self—body, soul, and mind—into the
hands of her Creator and follow His guidelines for her life,
all to His honor and glory.

There is more to self than understanding our sexuality.
You and I need to know who we are in all aspects of
life—soul, mind, spirit, emotions, and body.

Each of us has a real self and a false self. Our false self
is who we think we are, based on impressions we want
to leave with others. It's an ideal self. Our real self is how
others see us and how we really are. We must understand
our own real self before we can identify our false self, or
before we can remedy our wrong attitudes and habits.

What you say about yourself is more revealing than you
might like to believe. If you always comment about yourself, maybe you're just covering up something. "Oh, I'm
so busy. I just can't get everything done," may be a cover-
up for neglect.

Eugenia Price says in her book *A Woman's Choice,*
"The balanced woman who knows herself doesn't waste
time and energy on self-comment. With her own short-
comings and attributes well in hand, she goes on about
the business of living. She is not complacent, she is simply
free."

The woman who has a false idea of herself demands too
much of her family and friends. She's unable to recognize
her tendency to pity self, and therefore places unreal
demands on others.

She causes her family great hardships as she slaves at

her homemaking duties. She's full of self-pity, resenting the fact that they never thank her for what she does for them. Yet, it's a duty she *chose* to do. Why should they thank her? Does she thank the children for everything they do for her? Does she thank her husband for going to work every morning?

Some women demand too much of themselves because of their lack of self-understanding. They do all the work themselves. They think they are indispensable to their family and fail to teach the children to take responsibility. They think they want to work hard and care for the family. However, what they really want is for the family to be dependent on them. It's an ego-inflating method —although they may not be aware of it.

Parents who fail to understand self and real motives project their own unfulfilled dreams onto the children. Without realizing it, they use the children to further their own image of themselves. They never went to college, so the children *have* to go, even though they may not care about it. Mother insists that daughter be a nurse or a teacher or a missionary because she herself never realized her childhood dreams. Father insists that son follow his vocation—doctor, lawyer, farmer—yet the son lacks the interest and abilities. Children under such parental pressures cannot be true to themselves.

A schoolteacher who has never understood her real self is very unhappy. Her principal, who is aware of her real self, has assigned her to teach slow learners. She relates closely to them. She does a beautiful job because of her sensitivity, her empathy and identification with them, because of her own rejection in childhood. Yet, she's unhappy because she wants to teach the bright children, the fast learners. She refuses to understand her true self and lives in a false self-image in a make-believe world.

I've mentioned some life patterns of women who don't

understand themselves. You ask, "How can I learn to know myself?"

To some extent, every woman knows who she is. She learns this growing up in a family, in school, and in neighborhood play situations. People soon tell you who you are: "Don't be so catty!" "You're a poor loser." "You never do anything you don't have to." "You're always cheerful." "I like your humor." "You're brave." To some degree we know; yet too frequently we aren't willing to accept ourselves. At the same time there are some attitudes, motives, and images of ourselves we've never recognized.

You really *want* to know who you are—your true self—and you must know in order to understand yourself. You identify the real you through attitudes, motives, and goals—not through your status—married or single—or through your family, your job, or accomplishments.

You begin by resolving to be honest with yourself. Find a friend who will spend time helping you. (If you're married, let your husband be that friend.) Each of you write down three good things about the other person. Then have the other person write down one thing he doesn't like about you and wishes to see changed. You'll be able to accept one criticism in exchange for three compliments! One husband wrote, "I like the good meals you prepare. I appreciate the way you care for the children and how well you relate to them. I don't like the way you treat my friends when we're with them." This is growth when you catch a glimpse of yourself—of your true self.

By being honest and sincere in your self-evaluation, you'll recognize your abilities and accomplishments as well as your lacks and failures. It is not necessarily a sign of pride to recognize your abilities and strengths, while at the same time being aware of your weaknesses.

To run yourself down hinders you in doing what you can. In effect, when you belittle yourself, you are belittling God. He made you who you are—with your unique talents and lacks. To compare yourself with others is not good. Remember, you are God's unique original! What an honor and privilege it is to be designed by the Almighty God! He knows the end from the beginning. He never makes a mistake. He created you an individual—none other like you—for a purpose. He has a plan for you. Unless you know who you are and are honest with yourself before Him, you will not realize the fulfillment of His plan and purpose for your life.

Check your motives. Why do you want to change jobs? Is it because you want more prestige and power? Why did you accept that new assignment when you knew you already were too busy to the point of neglecting your family? Be honest.

Also check attitudes about any current issue, about society, government, church, family, marriage, God. Do your attitudes square up with those you want or think you have? Bring into your self-examination your ideas, wishes, likes, and dislikes.

Understanding self means you have a right concept of self-love. If you cannot have a healthy appreciation and love for yourself, you are unable to love others. Didn't Jesus Himself say that you should love others "as yourself"?

To be sure, there is a right and a wrong kind of self-love. The destructive kind is grabby, selfish, self-centered, thinking only of self, regardless of the outcome. I don't need to explain or go into detail. I know all about that kind of self-love already, and I presume you do, too. The right kind of self-love is a sincere, God-directed concern for one's self. Self-love motivates you not to knowingly poison or ruin your body.

Right self-love never hampers. The wrong kind pampers and expresses itself in self-indulgence, which, in all honesty, is self-hate. Many women complain about their situations, thinking that "greener pastures" exist across the fence. Their negative attitudes—self-pity, resentment, criticizing, and complaining—hinder their creative and positive contribution to their family, community, church, and work. They indicate self-hatred.

The right kind of self-love frees you to be concerned about others and helps you to deny self when it conflicts with the good of others.

You must also come to God, your Creator and Designer, and permit Him to convince you of your true self. As you come to Him, in sincerity and truth, He will reveal you to yourself.

How will this happen? Begin with an honest prayer, asking Him to show you who you are, and then open yourself up to His Spirit's probes. Allow Him to do this as you read His Word. In comparing yourself with His plan for His children, you quickly discover the difference between your real person and what He expects.

You can turn to almost any passage in the Bible and discover some truth about God and His plan for His creation. There are, however, some very pertinent passages that speed up the process—for example, the Sermon on the Mount (Matthew 5,6,7); the Love Chapter (1 Corinthians 13); or any passage in the Gospels where you find the life of Jesus. (We are supposed to be His followers.) Also note Paul's letters of advice and encouragement to the Early Christians.

As you read, have a receptive, learning attitude. Approach the Word with an open mind to hear Spirit truth and to understand how it relates to you. Come before Him with the honesty and freedom to accept, to believe, and to obey what He shares with you.

In Christ's parable of the talents, the man with only one talent failed to understand himself. He failed to understand God. He was a "fraidycat." He buried his talent instead of recognizing it and doing what he could. But that's all God desired of him—to do what he could.

Understanding self-love and which kind you have contributes to peace of mind and heart.

When you finish with your self-evaluation, hand yourself and just who you are over to Jesus Christ. Let Him fill your whole being with Himself and use you as a light and witness of God to others.

When you see yourself in Christ's presence, good things begin to happen. You'll be humbled, but like the branch the wind blows, you'll snap right back. According to Eugenia Price, in another quotation from *A Woman's Choice,* Christ seems to say, "Yes, that's pretty bad, but come on and walk with Me, My way. You'll be surprised at the places you and I can go together."

You are important to God! In order that His best plan for you can be completed, you must understand yourself. He'll help you.

Understanding yourself leads to peace and to rightness of the heart.

4
Self-acceptance

After self-understanding comes self-acceptance. Without this move, your understanding of self is worthless.

I recall a woman who could analyze herself perfectly. She was an expert at it—almost sounded like a psychiatrist. She had been to psychiatrists for a number of years, yet she couldn't accept herself and continued to be unable to cope with life. She understood who she was—her personality traits, her strengths, and her weaknesses. But that wasn't enough. She needed to take the next step of accepting herself and then move on to work at change.

Have you accepted yourself as God made you? I'm not suggesting a blind fatalism where you fold your hands and say, "That's just the way it is," or where you attribute everything to fate or to a "Higher Power," and you go scot-free from responsible actions! Not at all.

The acceptance I refer to is accepting the truth about yourself—your honest motives, attitudes, likes, dislikes, strengths and weaknesses, abilities and lacks, your potential.

It's accepting the truth about yourself and not stopping there, but moving on to work at wrong attitudes, wrong concepts, and sins. It's an honest acceptance of those qualities and abilities or lacks that you can't change, those things about yourself that you can't control. You're tall and wish you were shorter. You have blue eyes, and you always wanted dark brown eyes. You can't carry a tune, and envy the community soloist. You always wanted to lead but fit in best as a helper and supporter of the group you relate to.

When you accept yourself as you are, and quit demanding or dreaming about the impossible, you feel right with yourself.

Sophia became disillusioned with her marriage and family. She took up a full-time job without making adequate provision for the children. They are roaming the streets and creating problems for the neighborhood. Sophia is pretending that she is not a mother. She has not learned self-acceptance.

Only through self-understanding and self-acceptance can God make of you the person He wants you to become. After you recognize your real self, you can hand yourself over to God.

Without acceptance of self you can't work at what needs to be changed; nor can you hand yourself over completely to God. You limit His work in your life.

I'm so thankful that God doesn't ask me to be someone I am not; nor does He require from me that which I cannot perform. He requires that I turn myself over to Him and with His guidance and help be faithful and honest in doing what I can do.

At this point I must inject an important principle: We need to be selective and mature enough to choose from among many options and possibilities.

A lovely college graduate became very frustrated. She had many interests and had been successful in many areas. She had dabbled in archaeology, ventriloquism, drama, mass communication, and travel. She thoroughly enjoyed each one and proved capable and efficient. She set out to develop her full potential. She had never been confronted with the fact that she could not possibly develop her full potentials. She had too many. In conversation with her, I suggested that it was up to her to choose, with God's help, which to pursue. She should discern which potential He wants her to pursue and develop it for His glory. Whether or not she has chosen, I don't know. I do know that only in acceptance of this truth can she be right within. She must also accept the fact that choice produces limits. When she chooses, she eliminates the possibility of pursuing another career. A mature woman accepts the limits of her choice.

A denial of who you are, or rejection of self, hinders you from fulfillment, joy, and peace. You thwart growth— emotionally and mentally, spiritually and socially. An unwillingness to accept self keeps you defeated and critical. Sally chose to remain single, but she continually throws sarcastic remarks at her sister who chose marriage. Norma can't accept the fact that she has a facial disfigurement and isolates herself from family and friends. Sue is determined to win the club presidency but has no leadership qualities and makes life miserable for all of her associates.

Only a self-understanding and accepting woman can understand and accept others—parents, friends, colleagues, husband, or children.

It takes a self-understanding and accepting mother to raise children. A sickness early in life left little Kent with a physical handicap. His parents have worked hard to help him accept it and rise above it.

One day while his mother was reading to him, to her great surprise and joy, Kent commented, "I can't run. I can't jump. I can't play at recess, but I can read better than anyone in the class!" That was true. He had developed the ability to read and use words beyond a seven-year-old's vocabulary. This recognition and acceptance of himself was a result of his parents' efforts to help him to understand and accept self.

Self-acceptance is basic to right living. However, acceptance broadens beyond this concept to include acceptance in other areas. To be the person God intends her to be, a woman must also accept circumstances she cannot change. If her husband's job takes them to the city and she prefers the country, acceptance is the key to happy living. To complain about it constantly is disastrous to herself as well as to her husband and family. A woman needs to learn to accept sorrows, illness, disappointments, death, misunderstanding, and financial reverses as well as joys, successes, and delights, as a normal part of life.

When adversity strikes, remember: "Accept this. Only in acceptance lies peace—not in forgetting nor in resignation nor in busy-ness. His will is good and acceptable and perfect." Betty Elliot wrote this to her friend Catherine Marshall, who recorded it in her book *Beyond Ourselves.* It was her approach after her husband was killed by uncivilized Auca Indians.

Acceptance is the key to peace. It says, "I won't waste my time and energies fighting. I will accept this situation knowing that God, in His goodness and love, will make something good out of it." Such an attitude of trust and hope opens the door for God's creative plan to begin functioning. As long as there are negative attitudes of criticism, complaints, and self-pity, God's creative, positive plans cannot develop.

One hindrance to peace of heart and life is that we think life should be fair and just, that people will be grateful for our contributions, that they'll express appreciation. But I've discovered that no one can expect life to consist of "Flower-strewn pathways all our life through." In this life no one fully receives what he/she deserves. In acceptance lies the basis for a serene, peaceful spirit.

In her book *A Woman Doctor Looks at Love and Life,* Dr. Marion Hilliard states that "life holds one certain quality for everyone—suffering. This is to be expected. The extra bonus life sometimes gives is achievement. I would never wish anyone a life of prosperity and security. These are bound to betray." She believes one's approach to life makes it possible to live above the difficulties and unwanted situations: "Assume that life naturally is difficult, will never be easier. Accept the inevitables and live vigorously."

With this assumption, we can accept the difficulties of life as we encounter them daily. We accept these with faith in God's power of love to change and light the whole of life.

I want to conclude this chapter by referring briefly to a woman's acceptance of herself as female. I believe this is crucial to self-acceptance and acceptance of all of life.

In today's culture I find many women who fight being "woman." They feel cheated and discriminated against. They may feel that God has a spite on them or that they're missing out on life. Such attitudes hinder a woman from enjoying life and from being at peace with herself. Regardless of why she feels a lack of self-worth, she needs to move on to self-acceptance as a female.

Woman is created by God, in His image, for a unique purpose and role in society. As she accepts God's love and purpose for her and accepts Him as a personal Friend, she can accept herself and enjoy being a woman.

The woman who accepts herself and life's situations is capable of accepting the individuals she relates to in her own sphere of action—both in the home and outside it.

Self-acceptance—a key to peaceful living.

5
Peace Within

Within you and me there is an inner search for peace. Every living person longs for release from life's restless, dissatisfied feeling.

How do you find peace within your inner self? Some try to find peace through psychic power. Bob Hoffman, a psychic leader in Oakland, says he has developed a psychic-counseling method for emotionally disturbed persons which brings them and the people around them to peace with themselves. He did admit, however, that this was only temporary.

Transcendental meditation, the rage across our nation, brings peace of mind during the period one engages in it. It doesn't resolve the unrest which comes hours later.

Some try to find peace through all kinds of pills which supposedly remove irritations, work, worries, and wrinkles. It's a drugstore peace which soon wears off.

You've seen the advertisements promising happiness and peace. Mary starts screaming at the children. She builds up tension, gets angrier by the word. Then she reaches for the pill that promises the children a new mother. She may fall asleep—or shut herself up in a corner and forget about the kids.

Is that peace? Withdrawing from the cause of tension may be a certain kind of peace, but it doesn't resolve the problem.

Many women frequent doctors' offices trying to find rest and peace. A wealthy woman seemed on the edge of a nervous breakdown. She visited a nerve specialist. After some moments of consultation, the doctor advised, "Leave the city and go into the country."

"I do live in the country," she replied. "It's beautiful, with miles and miles of woods and hills and birds and fresh air about me."

"You need comfort, perhaps to be more relaxed. Travel more. Attend the concerts and theaters."

"But, Doctor," she responded, "I travel frequently and have attended concerts so often that I have grown weary of it all."

The doctor was strangely quiet. He looked serious, then admitted, "You've come to the wrong physician. It is a rest of soul that you need."

The doctor was right. There is only one Person who can give rest of soul and peace within. He invites, "Come to me, all of you who are weary and over-burdened, and I will give you rest!" (Matthew 11:28).

You cannot find this rest in psychic powers—not in pills—not in trying—not in circumstances—not in withdrawing from reality—not in things or pleasures. It's a free gift from God. There's no other way!

Saint Augustine wrote, "Thou hast made us for Thyself, and the heart of man is restless until it finds its rest in Thee!" Although this truth was spoken centuries ago, it is as true today as it was then.

Awareness of God, conscious or unconscious, is universal in humanity. It is the key to being human. A leading Austrian psychiatrist, Dr. Viktor Frankl, writes in his book *The Unconscious God* that much anxiety, neurosis, and discontent stems from the fact that a person's basic drive is to find meaning. The thesis of his book is that very deeply within "each and every man's unconscious depths" there is this religion sense. Religious faith is not an illusion or a crutch, as Freud taught.

Within each human individual there is a desire to relate to God, our Maker. He is a Spirit. Within each one of us is also a spirit. It reaches out to the Great Spirit God. But God is holy, righteous, and sinless. He cannot relate to anyone who has wrongness in his or her life.

We're caught with this concept of right and wrong. We desperately search for rightness in our hearts. We long for the ability to do right, the ability to refuse to do wrong. There's also a built-in regret for having done wrong. We make mistakes and miss God's perfect demands. Our sins separate us from God. There's guilt. There's fear. There's remorse. There's hate. There's frustration, tension, anxiety, and everything else related to such a state. This is good. It drives us to Him, for only a closeness to God can satisfy this cry of the spirit within us.

God has prepared a way for us to reach Him through Jesus Christ who died on the cross and shed His blood for our sins. Through this "new and living way," we can come back to a holy and right God and relate totally to Him (Hebrews 10:19,20 RSV).

The way to God and peace within is available to anyone. What must you do? Just believe (*see* Ephesians 2:8; Romans 10:9). By faith in God and Jesus Christ you can enter into God's presence and enjoy a close relationship with Him.

You confess your sins singly and sincerely to God, then accept His forgiveness and His "forgetness." Then you can forgive yourself—and forget. "If we confess our sins, he is faithful . . . to forgive us our sins, and to cleanse us from all unrighteousness" (1 John 1:9 KJV). "All" includes *any* and *every* wrong thing you've ever thought, spoken, or done. Praise the Lord!

His love forgives your wrongs and removes your guilt. His love enfolds you. He gives you peace. That restlessness disappears.

He shares His ideas and truths with you as you read His Word. You respond in love. You stay close to Him. You love Him, and you express it by pleasing Him in any way you can.

God gives you rest (peace) in the midst of any problem, illness, disappointment, heartache, sadness, change of plans, teenage rebellion, etc., as you bring each situation and need to Him. Through Him you can find the cure for tension, worry, and unrest.

When you face problems and difficulties, God promises to help. "Call upon me in the day of trouble," He says, "I will deliver you, and you shall glorify me" (Psalms 50:15 RSV).

In another passage, He tells how to keep from worries: Be glad you know Him. Remember that He is right beside you. Tell Him your problems in detail, with a thankful heart. The result? A peace beyond human comprehension (*see* Philippians 4:4–9).

What happens? You leave your situation in the hands of Almighty God. You now fill your mind with positive, good, kind, pure, and lovely thoughts.

His power enables you to rise above the wrong. However, you are still human, and sometimes you wander away from Him. You go your own way. You follow other people's ideas. You don't take time to evaluate what you read or hear or think—you don't compare it with God's ideas.

So you find yourself thinking, saying, or doing something which displeases Him. You lose your peace. But just that suddenly, as you recognize it's gone, you can again restore that relationship as you ask for and receive God's instant forgiveness (*see* 1 John 1:9). I like that instant product, don't you?

Now you are free! Free from restlessness within. Free from following selfishness and sin. Free to relate to a righteous God. Free to choose to please Him.

The guiltless, peace-filled heart is free to obey God and His truths and to obey conscience. The inner conflict between self and God is gone.

You now experience righteousness (rightness) in the heart. That's peace within!

Peace

With eager heart and will on fire,
I strove to win my great desire.
"Peace shall be mine," I said; but life
Grew bitter in the barren strife.

My soul was weary, and my pride
Was wounded deep; to Heaven I cried,
"God grant me peace or I must die;"
The dumb stars glittered no reply.

Broken at last, I bowed my head,
Forgetting all myself, and said,
"Whatever comes, His will be done;"
And in that moment peace was won.

                                          HENRY VAN DYKE

6
Peace of Mind

Did you know that more than half of our hospital beds are occupied by mental patients? Did you know that many women who regularly make appointments with doctors actually bring about their own illnesses?

Life gives these persons a bad deal. They can't cope with reality. Consider Dot, for example. She resents the move her husband's job required. She's in bed much of the time, and her children are frequently ill.

There are various causes for this type of problem, and we want to face them realistically. Let's look at some of the causes of mental and emotional illness.

Allergy to certain foods may cause physical disorders which, in turn, create mental illness. In *Quote* magazine it was stated that "British psychiatrist Richard Mackarness claims that as much as one-third of all mental illness may be caused by physical disorders—specifically, food allergies."

Some people believe there is a possible relationship between cancer and a person's state of mind. Although it's too early to take sides, they have noted in many cases that prior to the disease the patient had a strong feeling of despair.

The high pressure of today's life-style, advances in science and technology, and economic factors produce many changes. These may drive a man to take on more and more work and responsibility until he overworks physically. Tension, stress, and worry result, and may bring on heart attacks or other illness.

The modern woman especially is pressured. She's supposed to be capable of everything—both in the home and out. She's responsible to run the home. Her husband is absent much of the day and may work overtime or moon-light. She wants to be a sweet wife, loving mother, and helpful neighbor; yet her emotional upset rubs off on the family. Her husband comes home tired and worn out from bucking a hostile work world.

Emotionally they find progress hard to take. The soul and spirit can't keep up with the mind and body. It's almost impossible to find time to show love, to be con-cerned about each other, and to communicate. However, satisfactory relationships depend on sharing, caring, and talking things over.

It seems life is too busy for self-control, for learning how to handle anger. Bottled-up anger creates hostility, re-sentment, and hate. Uncontrolled anger leads to arguing and to pushing each other around. Such actions don't solve problems, they only complicate them.

Anger only sparks more anger. The woman or man who blows off and says everything that comes to his/her mind is not an honest person, as some modern authorities would have us believe. An honest person knows his/her feelings, identifies them, and surfaces them in a healthy manner. Verbal fighting and/or physical fights leave one with guilt feelings and leave the other person with hurts.

A broken home is the source of emotional problems for many children. Doctor Paul Popenoe, founder and direc-tor of the American Institute of Family Life, insists that "sound family life is the largest factor in mental health." This is true for both adults and children. A loving, peace-ful home atmosphere supplies a person's basic needs. An unknown writer states it so well: "One thing the human personality needs above all else is peace of mind, and the only source of such peace is a sense of love and being loved."

Such a home supplies a child's primary needs. He ex-periences wholesome relationships with a parent of each sex, and can identify closely with the one of his own sex. Mentally healthy parents raise children with healthy minds.

The person with peace of mind tries to deal with negative thoughts and feelings without hurting another. The unpeaceful person may try to escape reality through any one of many ways: illness, alcoholism, drugs, excessive reading, overwork, an overload of outside activities (even good projects), or by getting lost in pleasures. But these are momentary. They don't satisfy.

Although we need new drugs, new treatments, and new and better mental institutions, these are not the answer to peace of mind. The answer is in how you deal with stress and tension. This makes the difference between good emotional health or problems.

Sidney Katz, a journalist, author, and lecturer in the field of human relations, writes in the Canadian Airlines monthly magazine: ". . . Events related to your personal life make the greatest impact on your stress inventory." These personal problems include divorce, sexual difficulties, arguments with spouse, pregnancy, death, personal injury, illness, etc. The next category includes events related to your job or family, such as a change of job, change of schedule, interruptions, change in child relationships, or moving.

Mr. Katz believes that there's "no magic formula for relief of tension." You can never be completely free from stress. There's some stress in almost every human situation. This is true at home and at work. This need not be destructive or cause an emotional breakdown. Some stress and tension can drive you to a better solution, to achieve. The problem arises when stress accumulates and you seem unable to do anything about it.

To cope with stress, Mr. Katz gives practical suggestions he's gathered from mental health associations and interviews with doctors and psychiatrists. They work for most people, and he believes they'll work for you. I have adapted them as follows:

> *Talk away your tension.* Find some understanding, warm person and share your troubles, fears, and negative attitudes. (Also talk with God.)
>
> *Get away from it all*—but not permanently. That would only complicate matters. But take a walk, or sit in the park.
>
> *Do physical exercise*—walk briskly, do yard work, swim, hit a tennis ball, go bowling, play ball with the neighborhood children.
>
> *Take a good look at your work*—perhaps you're a perfectionist, demanding too much of yourself and your family. Or maybe you are too involved in outside-the-home activities. Look at your relationships with your husband and with each child. Maybe you need to work on these. Clear up misunderstandings by learning to communicate with your family.
>
> *Finally, don't worry about being tense.* That only makes it worse. Accept stress as a part of life, but focus on the positive.

Besides stress and tension, we need to deal with other negative feelings. Self-condemnation, self-punishment, and feelings of "I'm no good" soon give way to unhealthy attitudes. They result in an unhealthy approach to self, to everyone else, and to life in general.

Guilt feelings of unresolved sin not only weigh us down with wrong attitudes but also produce fear—of people, of the future, of consequences. Fear, in turn, produces tension and worry.

Christian psychiatrists agree that mental disturbance can be traced to some sort of evil working in the background. Some believe that mental illness is a result of the rebellion of the heart of man against the will of a perfect, holy God!

We know there are two powerful forces vying for your mind and for mine. We call them right and wrong—good and evil—or God and Satan. These two forces do affect our minds. We respond either to one or to the other. How thankful we are that God has made a way of resolving guilt through the death of His Son, Jesus Christ. All we need to do is believe, love, and stay close to Him and His Word.

There are two positive factors which contribute to peace of mind: praise and joy. The noted pastor Louis Evans, Jr., shares his remedy for overcoming migraine headaches due to stress and resulting tension. One night as he lay in bed with pain, the Lord seemed to speak directly to him, and suggested that tiredness is a result of doing more than He told him to do—or it was not taking God's strength to do it. Then the Lord suggested just to praise Him.

Mr. Evans obeyed. He praised God from "the prison of a foul attitude." His headache disappeared. Now when he feels a headache coming on, he praises God for all the lovely things in his life instead of focusing on irritations and negative thoughts. He sings. Without fail, his headache disappears.

What a beautiful formula: praise—joy—song!

God promises to keep anyone in perfect peace whose mind is stayed on Him—focused on Him and His truths (*see* Isaiah 26:3).

Peace of mind—a source of satisfactory personal relationships, of harmony in the home.

7
A Quiet Time

Too many adults avoid a quiet time—time to meditate and face themselves.

Many married couples aren't alone with themselves and each other long enough to define their goals for marriage and for parenthood. So they try to drown better knowledge and to avoid truth. They don't want to have to think about the present or the future.

Many homemakers have never taken time out from doing and hurrying to find their real selves. They forfeit their own true selves in order to be like others. They don't take the time or effort to think. They just accept what comes. Unquestioningly, they accept what the crowd, the printed page, or audiovisuals dictate.

I'm not advocating being an antisocialist or "copping out" in protest, but you can't enjoy relationships with others unless you bring to them of yourself. This calls for well-seasoned, rich resources of mind and spirit—all your own.

To know who you are calls for periods of apartness, for a time alone. We need time for thinking through why we do what we do: why we get irritated, depressed, or frustrated; why Susy is so fussy; why Bobby's grades have taken a sudden slide. We need to reflect on current housekeeping standards, on child-training philosophies, on teen trends. Then we can draw our own conclusions and discover who we are, our beliefs and true values of life.

Someone has said, "In the crowds there are many voices. In solitude only one." But perhaps in order to be yourself, that is the voice to listen to—that inner voice which is your spirit.

Where can you find periods of solitude and aloneness? At a retreat? During vacation?

I enjoy attending a retreat—getting away from daily pressures and responsibilities. I appreciate a vacation, too. It's also getting away. These are good, and necessary. But what about getting back to the mainstream of daily living? Can we carry back with us the rewards we enjoyed while away?

Karen spent a week at the beach. Her family was along, but much of the time they entertained themselves. It was such a relaxing week, and Karen made many resolves: She'd go back home and be less irritable. She'd be sweeter voiced, gentler mannered. She'd take time to listen and be more loving.

Then vacation ended and she found herself back home—meeting the family's needs, hearing their squabbles, soothing their aches, answering the phone, rushing to a part-time job, attending committee meetings. Before two days ended, she was her same old self—scolding the children, screaming her orders, tense, full of self-pity.

Why didn't Karen's vacation carry her over the rest of the time? She had a change from normal routine. She rested physically. She did have an escape from daily tasks, but not a release from them. She found rest, but not permanent happiness. Away from her tasks she resolved to do differently. But she returned with the same basic attitudes (mind-set) about herself and her responsibilities which she previously held.

Karen needed a change of goals, attitudes, and values rather than a change of responsibilities. She needed a change of focus—from self, to others; a change of resources—from her own capabilities and understanding to God's presence and power.

This process is similar to cleaning house. Once or twice

a year we clean everything thoroughly. But we also need daily cleaning. In the same way we need to clean out the dusty corners of wrong attitudes. We need to clean the linty accumulation of critical, unkind thoughts. We need to sweep down the webs of self-pity, of discontent, and of just plain meanness.

This can happen when we find peace of mind and tranquility. A vacation can't last for the remaining fifty-one weeks. We need to make a quiet time each day—a time when we get alone with ourselves and with God.

We can get snatches of aloneness in our daily routine even in the middle of pressures and difficulties. Our thoughts can escape beyond the routine of driving, outdoor work, of dishwashing, cleaning, and ironing.

We also need a longer segment of time daily. From this we receive inner strength and beauty of character, which enable each of us to better cope with occupational and family demands and privileges.

Constant activities and pressured schedules destroy a person emotionally, physically, and spiritually. We cannot do our best. We're unfair to ourselves, to family members, and to co-workers or neighbors.

Where can we find a quiet time?

It is quoted in *Family Circle* magazine that a noted author rediscovered himself by taking walks in the woods, in the countryside. He believed:

> Our best thoughts often come when we are alone in a quiet time. It is good to listen not to voices, but to the wind blowing, to the brook running cool over polished stones, to bees drowsing with the weight of pollen. If we attend to the music of the earth, we reach serenity. And then we can share some of it with others in some curious way.

You may not live close to the woods, but you can find some place—in your house, in the yard, in the park—and make that a place for a time of solitude.

Mothers through the ages have arranged this quiet time to suit their schedules. My husband's grandmother always knelt beside the beds as she made them and remembered each child by name.

Another mother would occasionally slip quietly up to the attic. For years the children never knew her mission there. But one thing they did know—she would come down from the attic with a radiant face and a new calmness!

One mother's usual custom was to step out of her door every evening at sunset and walk a few steps into her neighbor's orchard. The neighbor watched for some time, then accused her of trespassing. In reply, she wrote these words:

> I love to steal awhile away,
> From little ones and care,
> And spend the hours of setting day
> In humble, grateful prayer.

PHOEBE H. BROWN

She needed her quiet time! So do you. So do I.

In the stillness of your shut-off corner, you meet God in an invigorating, cleansing way. "Solitude is the audience chamber of God." In periods of solitude you can hear that wise voice of conscience, and God. To achieve as a person—regardless of your vocation—you need to include a quiet time in your daily schedule.

Set aside a time when you can be alone. It may be ten or fifteen minutes, or longer. It's best if it can be a regular time, but if not, don't let that hinder you. Meditation isn't enough. You need something to meditate upon. Take along the Best Book—the Bible. Read sentence by sentence. Reality and vision are brought into proper focus. You find truth. You rediscover yourself.

In your quiet time you remember that God is a Spirit. You worship Him with your spirit, in sincerity. Your spirits meet, in harmony. The Holy Spirit then moves in. Jesus illustrated the Spirit within as a flowing river of water.

We mothers and fathers need to find ourselves so we can help our children. We need to allow each child to develop his mind. This is necessary before he can be creative. His mind must have a chance to meditate, to be quiet, to daydream.

Give him a chance to lie on his back under an open sky and imagine characters or stories in the moving clouds. Give him a chance to stare out the window and think. Give him a vacation from radio and TV, from excursions and piano lessons. All are fine in their way, in moderation, but he needs time to think.

We see too few children sitting in the grass, feeling its cool dampness with their toes—or inspecting an anthill, or the petals of a flower. No, their time is often too crammed with activities.

Children need time to form daydreams of their own design, to have hobbies of their own choice, and conversations based on their own interests. They need time to wonder why, and then seek answers to their complex thoughts. The world of encyclopedias and libraries is imposed on them soon enough.

A child needs time to wonder and reflect on his purpose for being, to reflect on God. This brings faith to live by in a confused world.

Amid personal and family conflicts each of us needs that inner peace which comes through our quiet times with self and with God.

Each of us should daily pray:

Slow Me Down, Lord

Slow me down, Lord,

Ease the pounding of my heart by the quieting of my mind.

Steady my hurried pace with a vision of the eternal reach of time.

Give me, amid the confusion of the day, the calmness of the everlasting hills.

Break the tensions of my nerves and muscles with the soothing music of the singing streams that live in my memory. Help me to know the magical, restoring power of sleep.

Teach me the art of taking minute vacations—of slowing down to look at a flower, to chat with a friend, to pat a dog, to read a few lines from a good book.

Slow me down, Lord, and inspire me to send my roots deep into the soil of life's enduring values that I may grow toward the stars of my greater destiny.

AUTHOR UNKNOWN

8

Free to Love

A healthy mind is free to love—free from selfishness, negativism, and sin, which block the channel to the Source of creative love—the great Creator, God.

We freely use the word *love.* Oh, yes, "Love is the answer to human need," or "Love is what this old world needs," or "Love, not hate, fulfills all the law."

I've recently read about the discovery of a Stone Age tribe whose chief delight is to hurt or torture another. Suspicion, treachery, deceit, hostility, and fear are predominant in peoples who have not learned about love.

These traits are passed on from one generation to the next.

A noted doctor lists several emotions which produce disease in human beings. Fear heads the list. Next come frustration, rage, resentment, hatred, jealousy, envy, self-centeredness, and ambition. However, there is a remedy. The one and only antidote that can save persons from these is love.

Love is a small, four-letter word, but large in meaning. How it's applied today determines the future of mankind.

Wallace Friday said in *Quote* magazine that love is "basic in every marriage bond, essential in all lasting friendships, necessary in all relationships. . . ."

The need to love and to be loved is the simplest of all human wants. We can't live without it. No other need is so significant to our nature. It's as necessary and "compelling as the need for food," says anthropologist Ashley Montagu.

The most important influence in one's life is love, according to a research team at Harvard University which discovered some facts about love. The *Ladies' Home Journal* reported that the thousands of persons interviewed said that the love they received in their lives, now or in the past, was a major reason for their happiness now. Or the opposite was true—lack of love, now or in the past, was a source of present unhappiness.

Another interesting discovery of this research team was that family love was the biggest influence for contentment and fulfillment—above church, school, or any other factor. Doctor Pitirm A. Sorokin, world-renowned sociologist, stated that "no other agency or factor can compete with the family in the production of the intensest love and attachment."

But what if love hasn't been a part of your environment? Is it possible to learn to love? I believe it is. "But isn't behavior inherited?" someone might question.

Sociobiology presents the idea that you and I act as we do simply because of the kind of genes within us. The study of biological factors affecting social behavior in non-humans "includes a good deal of human behavior," according to Edward D. Wilson, professor of zoology at Harvard University, as quoted in the *National Observer.*

I am certain that some of my behavior patterns are a result of the genes I've inherited from my ancestors. There's no doubt about this. I also am aware that some behavior patterns I learned from my parents and brothers and sisters.

There's still another factor which regulates my behavior—my own will. This distinguishes me from being an animal. I'm a human being, created by God in His image. He gave me a will and a mind with which to make decisions.

I belive that I am responsible for my own actions. There comes a time when I choose how to act. To a large degree, I control my actions. The age when this responsibility begins is debatable—some say at the age of twelve, others place it later in life.

I can't hide behind my genes and my environment. I can choose, by God's help and power, to love others.

Love is difficult to define but not difficult to recognize.

Love is an affection which endears us to another. Love recognizes each person as a human being, made in the image of God.

Love is acting from a heart full of unselfish, outgoing concern for the other person. It's basically on the giving, sharing, serving side—not on the taking, quarreling, factional side. Love is not selfish.

Love is a gift. "God is love" (1 John 4:8), and unless He gives you this gift, you don't love.

We are motivated by God's love. It "requires no special feeling on our part. It requires only doing," writes author Eugenia Price in her book *Make Love Your Aim.*

Love is not so much a feeling as acting.

Love is sharing yourself with another.

Love is letting concern open up your heart to someone in need.

Love is listening to another's troubles and then feeling that they are yours, too.

Love is giving in at times rather than always demanding your own way.

Love is changing what needs to be changed in your life to please the one you love.

Love is forgetting about the hurt as time brings healing.

Love is focusing on the good qualities in another.

God commands us to love. Love is an act of the will. It is commitment first to God and then to the other person. That person may be a parent, a marriage partner, a business associate, a child, a boss, a neighbor, etc. It may even be an enemy—someone who doesn't like us.

Love produces love. We love God "because he first loved us" (1 John 4:19). We are drawn to Him by this power.

You learn to love as you draw from God's unlimited source, and, like Him, you can't contain it. You pass it on.

As Mrs. Lucille Stark of Houston, Texas, wrote:

Love

A man can own
uncounted gold
and land
and buildings tall

but love is just to give away
it can't be owned at all.

The heart that is right with God and with self is free to love.

9
Beauty of Character

When the heart is right and there's inner peace, then there is beauty of character. This is true beauty, not a surface or artificial beauty.

We see artificial flowers everywhere these days—in our homes, in business places, at stores, etc. They're attractive and call our attention. Sometimes they fool us into thinking they are real. But, upon close scrutiny, we can always detect their artificiality.

Artificial beauty is for sale, too. It focuses upon the folly of sham—to pretend to be something we are not. But genuine beauty cannot be bought. Surface beauty is often repulsive to us. We want the real thing, which is from within. It's an inner beauty that surfaces.

True beauty isn't dependent on physical attractiveness. Frequently in your evaluation of someone you begin by saying, "She is pretty, but . . ." and the continuation of that sentence is negative. However, if the person possesses qualities of true beauty, you will respond, "She's beautiful, and just as honest and good as she's pretty."

What you are, surfaces. It's reflected on your face. What's in the heart comes out. The face reflects the purity, peace, and joy in the heart. You can face people "eyeball to eyeball." You have nothing to hide.

Character is hard work. It doesn't come automatically. It's the result of achieving inner peace. A necessary characteristic is courtesy. Its roots reach deep into the soil of respect and appreciation—respect for everyone, without partiality. A courteous person appreciates the good in others and expresses it.

Honesty is another character trait of inner peace. Absolute truthfulness and honesty are a result of rightness in the heart. Honesty really is the best policy, even when the end result is unpleasant. You have to live with your own conscience—and to face yourself and God daily after you've deceived another can be worse torture than failure or bodily pain or financial loss.

Sandy was lab assistant at college. He belonged to a club which included some of his best friends. But they threatened to expel him from the club if he didn't reveal the chemistry test questions. At first Sandy decided to skip club meeting, then, on second thought, he realized that to do so would be cowardly. So, when the club president called for new business, he quickly stood and announced, "You don't need to throw me out. I resign. I didn't bring those questions. Besides, I never intend to be dishonest." Then he started to leave. But the boys pulled him back and by common consent dismissed the meeting and went to their rooms to study chemistry.

Sandy's decision came only after a terrific battle with his conscience and a determination to do right at all cost. He needed courage to carry through his decision. It was hard work!

Next, let's examine the trait of dependability. What do you think of the friend who says, "I'll meet you at 4:30," then doesn't show up until 5:00, or maybe even decides not to come at all. Maybe you're informed of changed plans; maybe not. Who is it that leaders and administrators contact when they need assistance? It's the one who finishes what he begins and doesn't think up excuses to get out of menial or difficult assignments.

And, like as not, when God hunts around for someone to carry out an important job, He won't take the quitter, the shirker, the on-the-minute clock puncher. He'll pick the one who has learned to do with all his might whatever his hands have found to do.

Another important character trait is purity. It isn't easy

to think pure thoughts with billboards, magazines, shows, TV, and books saturated with impure, immoral, indecent stuff! It isn't easy to be a "back number" when all around you persons condone illicit sex relations, immorality, and drugs. It isn't easy to refuse an invitation: "No, I can't see such a filthy movie," or "No, I wouldn't feel right at that liquor party." I repeat, it isn't easy. But I'll also add that it can be done. And it will be worth all the effort, prayers, and tears you'll need to stick to your decision!

Some forms of dancing incite passions and need to be avoided. It's what happens in one's mind that is harmful. Memories and thoughts do affect one's total being as well as purpose and goals in life.

How about smoking? Is popularity and acceptance by friends worth the nervous effects of nicotine—not being able to sit through a party or even a morning's church service? I've seen fellows go out of church just for their smoke. Is it worth the irritating cough—the possible lung cancer? And if you're a girl, who naturally expects to someday be a mother, is it worth denying your child its rightful heritage—a healthy body and mind and example? Our bodies are to be the temples where God's Spirit can dwell. He can't inhabit a dirty place.

Have you carefully and prayerfully approached the question of alcoholic drinks? Is the hangover worth the few exhilarated moments or hours? Think of the many drivers who are stimulated by just one drink and cause accidents and death. How about drugs—which are supposed to put you in touch with your real self? A right heart doesn't depend on any form of drugs for its kicks.

What do you think of the X-rated movies? I have in my hand a pamphlet written by a high-school boy. Only after he regularly attended the movies did he fall in with bad companions, start to smoke, to dance, and to keep late hours. Movies brought him under bondage. He'd skip

school, neglect his job, and even steal money to be able
to attend the movies.

Even after this young fellow gave his mind and life over
to the Lord, the effect of the movies wasn't easily erased.
"Movies did more to corrupt my thinking and provoke
temptations than any other influence upon my life," he
says.

Here's another area—your personal appearance. A
teenager recently said, "If you dress sloppy, you feel
sloppy. If you dress nice, you feel nice." By that she didn't
mean you have to wear expensive clothing or follow the
latest fashion. She meant wearing modest, decent clothes.

Excessive jewelry, outlandish clothing styles and colors,
extreme hairdos, and indecent exposure of body do not
make a girl or woman a person who is well thought of.
She may get wolf whistles and the attention of men of that
same type. But those men of honest Christian character,
the kind that lasts, will bypass her.

A friend of mine related that a certain insurance agent
refused to insure his neighbor's car because the teenage
son who drove it dressed sloppy and was dirty. The agent
commented, "Such a boy is a risk for our company."

Another important area is speech. A beautiful character
shows up in the way a person talks. There's a deep quality
of softness and gentleness. "A soft answer turns away
wrath" (Proverbs 15:1 RSV). The Bible says of a godly
woman, "in her tongue is the law of kindness" (Proverbs
31:26 KJV). This is true also of a godly man.

Words reveal character. Will Carleton has said, " 'Careful with fire' is good advice; we know 'Careful with words'
is ten times doubly so."

The story is told of a peasant woman who lived in the
Middle Ages. She had spread a false rumor about an individual in her community. Later she realized her wrong
and went to the village priest. She confessed her sin, then
waited to hear the penance assigned to her.

The priest said, "Take a bag of feathers, climb to the top of the bell tower, and shake them loose. Then collect them from the countryside and bring them to me."

The woman was horrified. "Oh, that's impossible. The wind will scatter them far and wide. I can never gather them all for you."

The priest replied, "Just so with your words; they can never be taken back again."

Words *are* important. They are a result of our thoughts and our meditation.

Our conversation with others reveals much about our character. A self-centered person will probably talk mostly of himself and his own interests, whereas a good conversationalist will introduce constructive, educational, and interesting subjects for conversation—and if he has nothing worthwhile to contribute, he'll not say anything.

Much of our conversation as Christians should center on God—His goodness and His many blessings to us. We will also share our experiences with Him through Christ. We will share the lessons He teaches us day by day. We'll converse about His promises which have proven true in our lives.

Our children will pick up our type of words and conversation. Grouchy, snappy parents will produce grouchy, snappy children. Nagging mothers will produce nagging daughters. Selfish, "I-inflated" stories will leave their traces.

The reverse is also true. When your husband tells you or you tell him, "I'm proud of you," your children will absorb this as a sponge does water. And it takes a bigness of spirit to praise another. Yet that's just what the youngsters will unconsciously learn—the bigness of spirit behind those words.

We need to guard our everyday conversations about the neighbors and friends. We show our appreciation of them by our conversations. By enlarging on the good in our neighbors and friends we are saying, "I'm proud of you." A mother once remarked that neighbor so-and-so ought to diet. Immediately her daughter caught her up, saying, "Well, maybe she is fat, but she has a lovely personality, especially with children."

"If you please," accompanied by a smile, changes an order into a polite request. "Thank you" is an outward sign of a grateful heart—grateful for the human side of family living, "for the little happinesses that highlight each day."

Words reflect patience, joy, love, self-control, kindness, and humility of inner character. For instance, just after you've waxed the kitchen floor little Nancy spills the glass of milk she is carrying across the room—something you have told her dozens of times not to do. Or it's five minutes before the children must meet the school bus and Tom left his only jacket out in the rain. Or you go to the refrigerator to get the pie to serve as a dessert, only to discover there are two pieces left instead of six. What do you say?

When Carl rushed inside the house pouring out his resentment because his friends were planning a camping trip and he had to stay home and help plant the garden, Mother said nothing. She waited until he had unloaded his mind. Then quietly and carefully she mentioned Dad's sickness and how thankful everyone would be for the lima beans and corn during winter days. Carl left the room a few minutes later, completely ashamed and determined to do even more than he had been asked to do.

A joyful, happy spirit belongs to a beautiful character. It's the joyful heart that can laugh at its own mistake and can focus on the positive rather than on the negative.

One mother dashed across the street to her neighbor's house one morning to get help with a dress pattern. A strange girl answered the door and invited her in. She discovered that the child's mother was in the hospital and her neighbor was keeping the child, Doreen.

Soon Doreen came skipping into the room waving a hairbrush. She sang, "If someone wants to comb me, I'll let them." The neighbor interpreted, "Doreen says that in her home they always sing their requests. Her mother says it's not so much what you say as how you say it."

What a difference well-chosen words, accompanied by joy and gladness, can make in our homes!

Is beauty of character your goal? Your thoughts and heart must be right, or you can never have those character traits that you really wish to possess. Daily you'll need to sort out the bad habits, the mediocre, the second best, and hand them over to God. He'll help you replace them with clean, honest, and pure thoughts and habits.

A heart that's right and a mind that's centered on God and truth produce a beautiful character.

10
Live With Joy

In the preceding chapters I've been focusing on various characteristics which are basic for experiencing rightness in the heart. Another one which deserves special attention is joy.

Can you identify with the words of the song I remember singing as a youngster, "I have a joy, joy, joy, joy, down in my heart"?

Do you find joy each day?

"You've got to be kidding!" Mary retorts. "With my noisy kids fighting all day long?"

Carrie sighs, "Joy? When all my children neglect me?"

"I work hard all day and come home to an empty house," says Jane. "That's not happiness!"

And John asks, "With all this competition I face every day, how can I experience joy?"

Nobody can make Jane, Mary, Carrie, and John happy. Nobody can give them a simple formula which is 100 percent effective, although there are helps.

Most of us equate happiness and joy, but I believe there is a difference. Happiness seems to be dependent on possessions, on pleasant situations, on a moment of pleasure, or getting what you want. I am happy when I receive a phone call from one of the children or when I get a new dress.

Happiness comes from something external.

Joy is an inner attitude not dependent on situations and things. It is not a natural characteristic, but joy can become a habit. You can learn to be joyful. And joy shared increases joy. Some lines from an old song put it this way:

> Share your joys, do not withhold them.
> Each one shared will sweeter be.

You as an individual can create an atmosphere and feeling of joy by your attitudes and actions.

To help cultivate joy, try this experiment when you get out of bed tomorrow morning: The first thing you do is look in the mirror, smile, and say hello to yourself. That will get you off on a jolly note.

Some homemakers play joyful music in the early morning. Others sing songs of joy and gladness. Do you know what this does to you and to the entire family? It sets an atmosphere, a mood, for the entire day. Joy is contagious.

Joy floating into the home during those early-morning hours gives Mom and Dad and the children a good start for the day. Sure, there will be some difficult decisions you need to make, some incidents that could be irritating, but making up your mind to be happy gives a different dimension to daily living—both for you and for everyone else in your day.

Another guideline is to practice looking on the bright side. Joy is a positive approach to each situation. Look for a constructive approach, for glad thoughts, words, and actions. When you're depressed, fearful, uptight, worried, or sad, look to God. Claim one of His promises. This gives you peace with yourself, with God, and with others. Joy flows from such a heart.

A joy within cannot be hidden. It causes you to overcome moments of worry and depression by singing songs of praise and thankfulness, by repeating Scripture verses, or by reviewing pleasant memories. You can laugh, smile, sing, and think positively in the daily situations and relationships with the family, neighbors, or friends.

Another help in finding joy is to have purpose in life—to have goals beyond yourself and the present, to be "other" centered. This springs from an unselfish life and from a heart at peace with self.

Knowing the facts and the demands of what you're about to do also helps put joy in each day. Through the years, I've received many letters from homemakers who never learned the skills of homemaking. Their mothers never taught them and they never took time to learn. Now they are confronted daily with housekeeping chores, with caring for a husband and children. They are swamped with work. They're frustrated, nervous, and tired simply because they don't know how to cope.

However, from some of these same homemakers I received letters some months or years later. Surprisingly, they conveyed a completely new life, a new joy. What has happened? They've learned more about themselves and about each family member, and now can enjoy everything related to them. They've learned the basics of their homemaking profession and are more relaxed. They've also discovered Someone who is by their side, helping them to face every situation. That Someone is God—the Source of inner peace, the Source of that inner ability to face each day and each situation with joy.

They live with joy each day. They enjoy the little things in their world—a smile, sunshine, health, a breeze flowing through the windows, the child's first steps, each new word, the smudgy kiss, a wink. They enjoy their home, the familiar objects and furnishings. They enjoy the relationship with each family member.

Ignorance and the unknown bring frustration and fear in every area of our lives. A successful vocation depends largely on being aware of what's required and being prepared. This is true for a successful marriage and parenthood. However, there's no excuse if one wasn't fully prepared. Any person can learn from all the available literature and seminars, from those with experience, and from God.

Many persons fail to capture today and its joys because their thoughts are focused on memories or dreams. Many parents either live in the past or in the future—when the baby comes, when they didn't have any children, when the baby will talk or walk, or how nice it was when he was an infant. Dad can hardly wait till son is old enough to go fishing or to help him in his business. Mom dreams about the day when daughter will help in the home or when she will be a young girl bringing her friends and dates home.

Some mothers and fathers are unhappy because they choose to focus on the negative. I was very disturbed to read recently that when columnist Ann Landers asked her readers "Would you have children if you had it to do over again?" Seventy percent of ten thousand parents who responded said no.

In reading their reasons I decided that the children were not at fault but that the parents had chosen not to enjoy the children. They chose to focus on the negative or on what they couldn't do. They weren't free to travel, to visit, to buy many things they wanted, or to pursue their own desires. Others were disturbed with overpopulation. Still others were neglected by their children.

I'm thinking now of quite a contrast to this negative response to having children. I recently visited with parents who had seven children. They were very young looking, ambitious, happy, and successful in their involvements.

We talked for several hours. They shared freely about their family and the fun they have together in creative play, daily work, worship, and traveling. They also shared some problems and conflicts they were working through. But what filtered through to me, loud and clear, was the joy which permeated their relationships with each other, with the children, and with God.

Joy produces contentment. You're not coveting *things* someone else has, because your joy comes from within.

In a happy home there will be laughter. Laughter is like a tonic. It's often relief for pain. At times it can be better than medicine. It's health to the body. "A good laugh is sunshine in a house," said William Makepeace Thackeray.

Laughter needs to be developed, and we should encourage it in the home—not laughter at each other's mistakes, at disappointments, or at physical defects, but laughter with each other as we pull out the humorous happening or make an observation.

A happy home experiences family fun. This also includes jokes—old ones as well as new ones. The family plays and laughs together while doing daily routine chores. Singing together or playing musical instruments adds joy. Sharing daily experiences around the supper table or at family council can also add to the atmosphere of joyful relationships.

Another aspect of joy in daily family living is having basic guidelines for behavior and responsibilities. There is a security in knowing the limits—what is allowed and what is not.

God is a God of order. He has given us natural, physical, moral, spiritual, and emotional laws. He's also given interpersonal laws which, if followed, help families resolve conflicts and enjoy life. If these laws are disobeyed, it spells trouble.

Joyful family living includes faith in God—a faith that brings God into daily thoughts, attitudes, and actions. "The joy of the Lord" is their strength. He, too, is the Source of love—the foundation on which to build joy in our lives. He helps us to be joyful through troubles, trials, and temptations. These are necessary for growth and maturity, and for strengthening our faith.

The psalmist says about God, "Thou wilt shew me the path of life: in thy presence is fulness of joy; at thy right hand there are pleasures for evermore" (Psalms 16:11 KJV).

A joyful family is a great advertisement for the Christian faith! The incident is told of a missionary family who had moved to a foreign country. One day a neighbor came over, politely introduced himself, and announced, "My family would like to join your church."

The astonished yet delighted missionary responded, "So you've heard the Gospel message?"

"No," he responded, "but we've heard the laughter in your home and observed the fun you have together, and we know you have something we don't have."

Such a family will be familiar with Bible reading and memorization, and prayer. They'll attend church services together. Belonging to a larger group such as the church gives opportunity for fellowship with others and gives roots and meaning to life.

Gladys Jenkins, staff lecturer of the Association of Family Living, says the key to happy family living is everyday kindness. That's a simple statement, isn't it? However, it's not so simple to carry out.

The parents who have peace within can be kind, tender, merciful, and forgiving. They respect God, each other, their children, and others outside the home. Any person, young or old, living within or without a family, can live with joy as he/she follows the pattern I have just suggested.

Loyalty to Jesus Christ brings joy to any person! Try it!

Live with joy today—not merely for a better life, but so that everyone you contact will be attracted to your God, the Originator of joy. The joyful person and the joyful family bring happiness to others.

Is your joy showing today?

Part 2

HARMONY IN THE HOME

"If there is beauty in the character,
There will be harmony in the home."

11
Love Between Husband and Wife

Harmony in the home begins with harmony between husband and wife.

God created man in His image—with basic male qualities and physique.

God created woman in His image—with basic female qualities and physique.

And it was good!

God planned marriage. It was His idea—not society's.

In marriage God intended that the two share together, complement and complete each other, help and fulfill each other in all of life. Together they live as equals in value, equal in their differences. Together, with biological differences and personality differences, they form a unit. They are together in goals and values but different in function.

The two become "one flesh" as they love each other and live for each other—in harmony. God designed marriage for the highest human happiness of one man and one woman.

There can be no harmony without love.

Love is the answer.

Love means different things to different people. The Greeks have four different words for love. *Eros* is the word for physical love or passion. *Phileo* expresses affection or a satisfied feeling, the kind of love you have for a friend or brother. *Stergo* indicates that quiet and abiding feeling when you're close to someone and are satisfied with this recognition, such as the love of parents for children, children for parents, and the love of husband and wife. *Agape* is selfless love. Someone has defined it as "being aware of the other's need and meeting it when it's within your power to do so." Marriage, I believe, incorporates all four words pertaining to love.

Marriage is a love relationship—not a competitive game where the husband and wife each try to win in wit, will, and work. It is not a contract or "I'll do so-and-so if you. . . ." Marriage is not a relationship of law—fifty-fifty. Sometimes it may be a twenty-eighty or zero-one hundred. It's give-and-take because the man and woman love each other.

Love is more than feeling. Most often it is words and actions. Feeling may be there, but love doesn't depend on it. Love is basically an act of the will.

In the courtship days and early marriage, the feeling of love is very evident. Because of this it's easy and natural for a husband and wife to speak kind, endearing words and to enjoy physical love. It's a joy to meet each other's needs; to change one's own plans for the sake of the other's interests; to spend a lot of time doing things together. And rightly so.

However, with the pressure of jobs and the daily schedules; with financial problems and trying to get ahead; with today's emphasis on independence and success, a couple gradually spends less time together. Perhaps they only see each other at the end of the day when both are tired and perhaps frustrated by the day's events and problems. Perhaps their attitudes about each other and about their roles and functions have changed. And because that feeling isn't there, they soon fail to act in love.

In order to insure peace and harmony in the home, God gave a few guidelines (*see* Ephesians 5:21–23). The husband and wife are to share together, to communicate with each other, to love each other, to show kindness and mercy, to be kind and forgiving. He also knew that in such intimate relationships, conflicts and differences would arise, so He suggested they "submit to each other."

Together they should share thoughts and feelings and ideas, even if they differ. They say, "If that's what you want, it's all right even though I can't agree," or "You know best." But what if they stalemate—*both are right?* God suggests that for the sake of harmony the wife should submit to her husband, "as unto the Lord." It's an act of obedience to her Lord.

Marriage is an institution, and as such God designated that the husband assume leadership and responsibility to see that everyone's needs are met. He in turn answers to the headship of God through Christ.

Interestingly enough, God's first specific assignment to the husband is to take leadership in bringing love and understanding to the relationship—a sacrificial, self-denying love which expresses itself daily in words and actions.

A husband could never become a dictator, tyrant, or bully if he follows God's commands to love his wife "as Christ loved the church and gave himself up for her," to love her as his "own body" (*see* Ephesians 5:28 RSV).

Surrounded by such an atmosphere of kindness, goodness, compassion, understanding, acceptance, and consideration, it's easy for a wife to respect her husband, to communicate her feelings, to submit in their disagreements, and to support his goals and interests. To love each other is not a harsh command. It can be exciting and rewarding.

What qualities does this self-sacrificial love demonstrate? Let's see what 1 Corinthians 13 (the Love Chapter) has to say:

"Love . . . is slow to lose patience—it looks for a way

of being constructive." This means being patient when the husband invariably is late for dinner or when the wife is still dressing and it's time to leave for the appointment. It's constructively using those few minutes in prayer, in reading to the children, or in cleaning up the counters.

"*Love . . . is not possessive.*" It is not jealous. She does not show resentment when he is the center of attention, nor does he demand taking the lead in conversation. Love rejoices in the other one's abilities and acceptance.

Love . . . is neither anxious to impress nor does it cherish inflated ideas of its own importance." Neither one delights in saying, "I told you so." Nor do they laugh in public about each other's faults or correct each other's speech.

"*Love has good manners.*" A wife speaks courteously to her husband. He is polite in actions and in speech—as during the courtship days. Love notices what the other person wears and does—expresses appreciation for the daily favors and kindnesses—listens attentively when the other one speaks—respects each other—highlights the good qualities and minimizes faults. Love covers a multitude of faults.

"*Love . . . does not pursue selfish advantage*" to the neglect of the spouse's needs and interests. Love will be willing to give up personal wishes, "rights," or plans when it is best for the children and husband or wife.

"*Love . . . is not touchy.*" It does not take offense at some well-meant but perhaps negative-sounding remark. She won't pout if he fails to notice her new dress; he doesn't resort to angry silence if she disagrees with his opinion. Love isn't irritable. It tries to understand the reasons behind the other's actions or reactions.

"*Love . . . does not keep account of evil.*" In their disagreements they stay with the issue and don't dig up all the hurts and wrongs of the past. Each keeps in touch with the other by sharing personal feelings and not accusations.

"Love . . . does not . . . gloat over the wickedness of other people . . . it is glad . . . when truth prevails." The wife who truly loves her husband is not glad when he is hurt, even by his wrongdoing. He doesn't allow bitterness in his heart. They forgive and forget all wrongs, knowing that hostility is a deadly disease, as fatal as cancer. It spreads into every area of daily living until it kills the marriage.

"Love . . . knows no limits to its endurance." Agape love doesn't say, "I can't stand it any longer! I give up!" Love is long-suffering and patient.

"Love knows . . . no end to its trust." They continue trusting each other. She accepts his reason for being late and does not imagine he's deceiving her. He isn't suspicious of her when he's gone all day.

"Love knows . . . no fading of its hope." Every morning is the fresh hope that the love and concern they knew in early marriage will be experienced again. As long as there is life, a wife hopes for her husband's complete love, respect, and concern. He hopes for her complete love and respect.

"Love . . . can outlast anything." In sickness or health . . . for better or worse . . . through joy or sorrow. This *agape* love is not their own brand. It comes from God. It is available for the ones who want it, who remain close to—in union with—Him and love Him with all their thoughts, emotions, desires, will, feelings, and bodies.

Billy Graham once stated that among the couples who have faith in Jesus Christ the divorce rate is one out of every five hundred marriages in contrast to the average ratio of one to three.

Jane and Harry were planning a divorce. Down deep neither one wanted it, but Jane just couldn't take any more from him. She confessed, "I don't love Harry anymore! I hate him. He comes home tired and frustrated each evening and in a bad mood. One evening he didn't like the meal I had prepared and threw it on the floor. I don't feel like being kind. Why should I be?"

Her friend challenged Jane to act out love. "But," Jane questioned, "isn't that being a hypocrite—if I don't feel like it?"

"Not at all," responded the friend. "It's the same as getting up in the morning. You may not feel like it, but you do it because it's the thing to do."

Jane grasped the truth. She returned home resolved to put love into action.

Two weeks later when the friend met her again, Jane was radiant. She exclaimed, "I've been acting out love. I have been answering his unkind remarks with kindness. It's true that 'a soft answer turns away anger.' When he's tired I try to be understanding and not make a lot of demands. I really listen when he talks. He shares with me again. I've been doing the nice things he likes—the way I used to when we were first married. He's started paying more attention to me and he tells me what he appreciates—the way he used to do. We don't talk about divorce anymore—and last weekend he wanted to go on a minivacation. It was beautiful! I've learned to really love him!"

Agape love wins every time. It never fails! It's the only road to peace and harmony in the home, and it begins first between husband and wife. They are living examples—models—of how love acts between two persons. From them the children learn how to love.

When there's harmony in the home, there's order in the nation.

12
Parental Unity

Parental unity is basic to a child's security. This is of tremendous importance and cannot be overemphasized.

I'm sure we all agree that children need parents, or parent substitutes, who love them very much, with a wise and caring love. They not only should love the children but they should also love and respect each other. Without a happy home it is almost impossible for children, in adulthood, to cope with either failure or success.

Parenthood is a privilege as well as a serious responsibility. We have a task no one else can do for us.

Our task is to prepare our children by guiding them to true values and attitudes of life. This means we need to help them understand themselves better—their drives, feelings, and needs—to help them accept their roles which they will assume in later life in their own families.

Material benefits aren't enough. To learn about child psychology and child management is not enough. Psychologists say that more important is the "outgoing, overflowing, undemanding love which is generated within a really happy marriage." To know that parents truly love each other and want and love him is a firm foundation for the child. With such knowledge, he can face life confidently and courageously.

He grows and develops; his affections broaden out from the family to include others. He is not born with true feelings of affection. The parents are responsible to help him acquire them.

Real affection isn't built by granting a child's every wish. It's the result of shared experiences and a comfortable relationship in which *persons* are important rather than *things.*

Doctor David R. Mace, the well-known marriage counselor, states in his book *Success in Marriage* that the parent who has arrived at a workable philosophy of life, has welcomed the child, and enjoys a satisfactory relationship with a mate, expresses affection naturally to the child. Parents who are unsatisfied in areas of their living either give the child "smother" love or ignore him.

Too many dads and moms don't realize the importance of parental harmony. They continually quarrel or throw barbs at each other. They criticize, or disguise resentment and hostility in satire or in jokes about each other. Children soon sense this attitude.

It's important for parents to agree on the rules and limits for their children. They need to present a united front to them. In this way, the children learn respect for their parents.

Parents must exercise firm, consistent, and loving controls in the home. At times they may be overstrict, at other times too lenient. The child can adapt to these moods. But when parents don't agree, then the child begins to manipulate them. He learns to play one parent against the other to get what he wants.

This is human nature. However, it only leads to problems when a child learns to manipulate his parents. This causes him to lose respect for them. It can wreck their marriage relationship, too, as each tries to win the child's loyalty. A competitive spirit hinders love and tenderness.

Many children suffer emotionally when parents oppose each other and are not united. The mother of a twenty-five-year-old hardened criminal poured out her anguish as she revealed that "the basic cause of his behavior was that his father and I disagreed about how to raise him."

Even if parents don't see eye-to-eye in their dealings with the children, they can support each other. Later, when alone, they can discuss their differences. To argue in a child's presence disturbs him emotionally. If they do argue in his presence (never on a subject related to him), they should explain that they do love each other but are only trying to decide on the best way to accomplish something.

If a child is to become a responsible adult, he needs to respect the laws of the school, church, and country. This he learns in his own home only if he has learned obedience to parents. He can be taught this principle early in life in a positive way: as parents help him carry out a command; as they praise an act of obedience; or, when necessary, as they punish.

Parental disagreement about how to discipline the children doesn't necessarily happen because they hold different opinions or theories; it's basically due to marital conflict between them. The control of the children becomes a battleground as Mom and Dad hit out at each other through the child.

By the time a couple has children old enough to present discipline problems, they should know each other's minds. When there's real love and affection toward each other, they will have arrived at a common philosophy of life and harmony.

That doesn't mean they have detailed plans for child rearing. Their basic attitudes of life largely determine their views about handling children. Parents identify with their children and want the same things for them which they themselves want. They may read books about child training but will only apply those methods which contain the basic principles they accept for themselves and their relationships.

The husband and wife who together arrive at common values and goals will express them in a united effort of child rearing. They will want to share their warm relationships and satisfying experiences with their children. This creates an enjoyable family circle of love for each other. Dad wants each child to love Mother as much as he loves her. He'll try to avoid any situation that will belittle her. Mother wants the children to love Dad as much as she does.

However, if they have not achieved warm and tender affection in their relationship to each other, they'll reproduce all their unresolved conflicts in their approach to their children. It's impossible for them to use the team approach as parents without being a real team as marriage partners.

When there is lack of unity and parents disagree about their children, for the sake of peace one of them is likely to withdraw completely from the scene and hand it all over to the other.

Out of Dr. Mace's many years of marriage counseling, he states the startling truth that he has never seen a serious parenthood problem that was not based on an unresolved conflict in the marriage. Furthermore, when parents resolved the marital conflict, the parental conflict disappeared.

He then concludes: "The solution to the parenthood problem lies in the solution of the marriage problem."

When a couple achieves harmony and peace, it's not just their own happiness that benefits. They'll actually help their children as much as, or more than, themselves. God knew best after all when He designed that the "two become one."

A child needs to experience loving relationships, because in this way he learns how to relate to others. He learns by example.

Parents should stop blaming the children and with the help of the Holy Spirit take an honest look at their marriage. Then they need to allow Jesus Christ to make them the parents God meant them to be—united in Him and each other—for the sake of helping their children learn about God, about love, peace, and harmony at home.

13
Children Need Love

Family living is intimate interpersonal relationships. Each person is different, with his/her unique personality, likes and dislikes, strengths and weaknesses.

To live together in such a close daily relationship isn't easy. But it is possible to bring into the family those qualities that help bring about peace, harmony, and joy. It requires much effort, understanding, and love.

Love is the most important element in family relationships.

Love is the one basic gift every child needs. Education, food, money, fun, and freedom from fear are good gifts—but love is better.

And "the most favored children in the world are the ones whose parents love each other," says Dr. Charlie W. Shedd in his book *Promises to Peter.*

A lot happens in the close emotional interchange at home. Nobody knows exactly what. But it's a known fact that hostility and bitterness between two persons spill over into the lives of those who are around them—and so does love.

Doctor Shedd relates in his book that at the Shedd home one time the children pressed the parents into saying whom they loved the most—each other or the children. The parents finally answered, "The love of a parent for a child is different. But . . . there's no stronger love than ours for each other."

One of their children said that when he heard this statement it seemed that his world was coming apart, but after he thought it over he "felt like everything fit together again good."

All other emotions come naturally to a child—anger, hatred, resentment, sadness, jealousy, sorrow, etc. Only love has to be learned—and from whom do you suppose God intended a child to learn love?

Parents show love in the way they talk to a child, handle, fondle, and caress him. The child feels their love. He senses their attitudes. No parent can fool a child by mere words or by actions if inwardly there is rejection, resentment, or preoccupation with other "more important" demands.

Love is shown through a mother's tenderness—a father's smile—fondling of the child—reassuring words—protection from danger—expressing appreciation—speaking kindly after he makes a mistake—accepting him into their hearts and lives, just for who he is—happy times together—firm, consistent guidance—understanding his feelings and desires—meeting the child's basic needs.

A mental-health bulletin prepared by the National Association for Mental Health suggests that children need "good food, fresh air, exercise, and plenty of sleep" in order to grow healthy and strong. They also have emotional needs. To grow up with good mental health, every child has basic needs which must be met. Every child needs:

> *Love*—He needs to feel that his parents love, want, and enjoy him, and that they care what happens to him.
>
> *Acceptance*—He needs to believe that his parents love and accept him as he is, although they don't approve of everything he does.
>
> *Security*—A child needs to know that home is a good, safe place and his parents are there to help; that he belongs to a family; that he's needed and can contribute to family work and play.
>
> *Protection*—He needs to feel that his parents will protect him from harm and help him face new, difficult experiences.

Independence—He needs to be able to grow up slowly, to try new things and have his parents' confidence in him.

Faith—Every child needs to have a set of moral standards to live by, and he needs to believe in human values—kindness, courage, honesty, purity, goodness. He needs to know God, the Source of these.

Guidance—He needs friendly help in learning how to relate to persons and things, mostly through parents' example.

Control—Every child needs to know that there are limits to what he can do and that his parents will hold him to these limits. They will let him know it's all right to have angry and jealous feelings, but he will not be allowed to hurt others or himself when he has those feelings.

According to the National Association for Mental Health, "Children whose basic needs are satisfied have a better chance to grow up in good mental health and to become mentally healthy adults—people who are good workers, good citizens, good neighbors, good mates, and parents." Love motivates parents to meet the child's basic needs.

Parental love forgives the children's mistakes and accidents. Parents do not hold these against the children and will help share in the costs when replacement or restitution must be made. Mercy—undeserved favor—is one of the attributes of God. Christian parents are models to show in a measure what God is like.

Forgiveness is a very important lesson in learning how to love others. We need God's help because He is the Source of forgiveness, mercy, and an unselfish concern for others.

Children learn how to love as they see love in action. Surrounded by love, the child responds with love. This is one of life's greatest searches—to receive and be able to give love. When denied love, life is tragic.

In my younger days I observed a mother who never had one good word to say for one of her sons. I observed his great embarrassment when in his presence she told us how clumsy he was and that he couldn't do anything right. The boy never had a chance. He didn't learn to love himself and was unable to love anyone else.

When father and mother love each other, the child isn't preoccupied with worry and fear. To him life is good. He expects the future to be good, also.

The child of quarreling parents usually feels guilty. He begins to think he's the cause of their conflict. He worries about what he has done wrong.

The child of parents who love each other also has a better chance sexually. At certain stages in his life a child has secret dreams and plans about the opposite parent belonging to him/her. A girl may want her father all to herself. The boy sees his dad hindering his love for his mother. It's just the way God made human beings. However, when the children realize that their parents love each other, making it impossible to claim them, they can move on in their own natural development. When this doesn't happen, confusion results. Here's where homosexuality, lesbianism, and other twisted sexual practices originate.

Parental love disciplines. By that word I mean to train the child by "instruction and exercise," to teach him obedience and order by "training and control." Unfortunately, most people think discipline means punishment. It may, as a last resort, when the child fails to respond to positive methods.

Obedience and all acceptable behavior is easier for a child when parents approach discipline with a positive approach. It's verbalizing their love many times a day. It's expressing love with an unexpected hug or smile. It's sympathizing with the bumps and scratches of everyday living, with emotional hurts and disappointments. It's little surprises along with rules and limits and warnings in order to save him from unnecessary hurts and fears.

Discipline develops self-control. Parents teach self-control as they "ask for obedience with quiet firmness in the essentials."

What are the essentials?

According to psychiatrist Richard Canfield, there are four essential areas. Parents should discipline in these four areas: 1) harmful to self, 2) harmful to others (or destructive), 3) disobedience, and 4) what they can't afford.

If parents disciplined in these areas instead of merely giving vent to feelings, they would have happier family living!

Parental love understands each child's individual personality. Love treats children fairly—although it may not be identically. It may be a model car for one child and a ball glove for another—according to individual preferences. It's identifying with the child's feelings of hurt and sorrow, anger and joy. It's a love that is available to meet the child's needs.

Every child needs love. It's his peace—his joy—his security.

14
Resolving Family Conflicts

Every family has problems and conflicts. Struggles consist of relating to each other, of satisfactorily working out everyday routines, of meeting each person's needs. There

are problems with children at different ages and stages
—involving money, health, friends, responsibilities, tragedies, accidents, death, etc.

Surveys point out that successful families have problems identical to those of unhappy families involved in
open conflict. The difference is that happy families learn
to work through their conflicts as they surface. They learn
to face the situation honestly. They try to resolve their
differences and arrive at a satisfactory solution for all.
They're interested in harmony in the home.

When family problems arise in your home, do you tend
to blame someone else? Do you try to resolve conflicts
with angry words, physical attacks, or the silent treatment? None of these really are solutions. They only create
more problems and conflicts.

The key to resolving family conflicts lies in the husband-
wife relationship. How do Dad and Mom face their problems? If they are able to resolve their differences in a good
way, they are supplying a positive example for their children to follow.

Henry would "burn up" every time he came home to
a littered-up house. His wife, June, knew this. At first she
reacted negatively. After all, what did it matter—some
magazines and a book or two on the floor, a pair of slippers
in the middle of the room, a table full of clothes that
needed to be folded. At least they were clean. He should
appreciate that!

June always defended herself: "I don't think our house
is a mess. You ought to see my sister's house!" They'd end
up arguing, followed by the silent treatment. After several months, Henry stayed away more and more with
excuses such as "I have extra work at the office," or "The
fellows want me to go out with them."

Fortunately, June realized what was happening. She
really did want to have a home he'd be happy to come

to. So one evening when both of them were in a good mood she asked him directly, "Honey, are you staying away because you can't stand an untidy house?"

To June's straightforward confrontation, Henry responded honestly, "I'm afraid so." He then proceeded to discuss his feelings. June expressed hers also and admitted her I-don't-care attitude. Henry admitted he was too much of a perfectionist. They both asked forgiveness and pledged their willingness to cooperate with each other. Their love for and desire to please each other were greater than personal preferences.

That was the beginning of a change. June needed help to know how to keep house. A close friend gave her some simple, helpful tips: Have a place for books and magazines and return them when you're through reading for the day. After you kick off your shoes, put them in a corner or under the couch. June put a table in the laundry room where she could dump the clean clothes that needed folding. She also planned a daily schedule. She was glad she did. She needed this experience before the children came—when it was even more difficult to keep a tidy home. Henry became more cooperative. He helped her when he could.

Several guidelines helped Henry and June resolve their conflicts. Any couple can use these guidelines in their own particular conflicts and struggles toward compatibility. They are also applicable in resolving conflicts between them and a child, or any other person.

1. Admit there is a conflict.

2. Look at the problem when both are in a good mood, if possible.

3. Honestly share feelings about the situation.

4. Stick with the issue at hand. Don't dig into the past or start attacking each other.

5. Lower your voice.

6. Find a positive approach for yourself rather than for your spouse.

7. Be patient through the struggle of changing behavior patterns.

8. Cooperate with each other through the problem.

9. Be interested in the happiness and welfare of each other.

10. Affirm your love for each other.

For some couples, guidelines aren't sufficient. They may need to confide in another person—a trusted friend or a pastor—in order to arrive at a satisfactory solution.

If a couple cannot reach agreement on the issue after honestly sharing feelings and needs, one may find the solution by giving in 100 percent in supporting the other's wishes. Love is the basis for resolving conflicts. Love cares. Love wants to please, not demand. Love doesn't limit either husband or wife to the fifty-fifty basis: "I gave in last time. It's your turn now!" That's law, not love!

I believe God intended the home to be the laboratory of life. There the child *learns* how to live with others. Brothers and sisters and parents form a little community, a miniature world, where together they practice the lessons of life. When there are no good models, where there are only bitter quarrels and fights, couples often separate and the children scatter and may become delinquents. Children need models to show them *how* to work through conflicts.

Where there are brothers and sisters, there are bound to be some fights, jealousy, and competition. Johnny teases Susy. He pokes her in the ribs or pulls her hair. Susy tries to get even and trips him. Each child knows what irks the other one the most. That's why God gave children parents—to help them learn to share, to care, to confront;

to cope with negative, selfish feelings and desires and to enjoy living.

Caring parents empathize with the child and identify with his feelings. They understand his needs. The famous child psychiatrist Dr. Haim Ginott was quoted in an article in *Family Circle* magazine as having said, ". . . a sympathetic statement of his [the child's] feelings and a dignified request are more effective than name-calling and threats."

Johnny is angry. He hits his brother who snatched his toy. His parents should catch Johnny's eye and say, "That makes you angry. It isn't nice when someone grabs things away from you, but you can't hurt your brother. Now go outside and kick the ball as hard as you can. When you feel happy, come back in." This approach allows the child to express his feelings without doing whatever he wants to do.

Should children be kept apart, engaged in separate activities, and each have his own space where the other can't invade? Often the best approach is to let them alone. Bickering, wrestling with each other, and teasing among siblings seem to be cured only with age.

At the same time, I do not believe that parents should never interfere. In those early years, parents should show children kindness and gentleness and how to share. Show them how to respect each other's possessions and how not to hurt or destroy. Then begin at about four years to stay out of their quarrels as much as possible. Make them responsible to settle their own disagreements. If this is not done, they soon learn tactics to get the parents' attention against a brother or sister.

As parents, we must try to be fair with each one, at the same time explaining to the child that life isn't always fair and equal.

Brothers and sisters often try to get even with each

other. This will lessen as you show them how to express their negative feelings correctly. Handling negative feelings in a positive way is a preventative measure. It reduces conflicts.

Authorities say capturing the child's visual attention when you talk to him helps you to communicate more effectively.

Frequently a child creates a fight just to see Mom come running and get all upset. So, Mom, if you do investigate, keep your cool. If necessary, ask questions and give direction, but be nonchalant about it.

There's also the situation when the new baby arrives. The kind of relationship that develops between the baby and the older child sets the stage for later interaction. The child should be prepared beforehand.

Resolving conflicts in a positive way is demanding. It takes more time and effort than an iron rule of word, or punishment. This latter approach only results in more and greater conflicts.

There are times for discipline and punishment when the child fails to obey, but these should be kept at a minimum. If not, punishment is useless.

There are times when you need to resolve a conflict immediately. When an older child is involved, an effective approach to resolving a conflict is to bring it to the family council. The younger children may not be involved, depending on the situations under consideration. Talking over the conflict, with each one airing his/her feelings, both negative and positive, and ideas about possible solutions, is very good. Although they listen to and consider the children's ideas, parents will make the final decision.

Parents and children can never see a situation from identical viewpoints, for each brings a different set of influences, wishes, and feelings to the situation. But with respect for each other as people, with politeness and love, they can live together in harmony. When there's good communication between them, they can arrive at satisfactory solutions.

Families need to admit mistakes and ask each other's forgiveness. This brings healing when other solutions fail.

Family is parents and children interacting and relating happily to each other. That's a part of growing up. It's learning together to resolve their anger, jealousy, wanting to get even, etc. Families don't have to continually fight and hurt each other.

With faith and love for God and each other, family is beautiful!

The Christian family learns to pray for understanding, for love, forgiveness, and kindness. Prayer is not a cop-out from the procedures I've mentioned. Never! But it gives an added dimension when you consciously want God's love, kindness, understanding, and wisdom added to yours. You realize He's got the answer to every conflict and wants to reveal it to you—but you have to take the initiative and extend the invitation for Him to do so.

He helps you live out the Golden Rule—to relate to others as you want them to relate to you. He helps you go the second mile.

Such relationships develop harmony in the home.

15
To Forgive Is Divine

Love is born of forgiveness. The two are as close as Siamese twins. You can't have one without the other.

Forgiveness is the cure for resentment, grudges, hostility, anger, revenge—any and all negative feelings and actions. We have a tendency to allow these bad feelings and thoughts toward others to stack up. But we can't have all these feelings and love at the same time. We need to clear our hearts and minds of these negative attitudes to make room for love.

It's a natural human tendency to make mistakes; to do or say the wrong thing; to be discourteous, thoughtless, and unkind. But forgiveness isn't natural. Like love, it has to be learned—and, like love, it should be spontaneous.

Forgiveness helps you. Anger interferes with the body's normal functions. It causes both mental and physical distress. The person busy cultivating grievances can't enjoy life. Even when you think anger is justified, the result is only bitterness and more frustrations.

A forgiving heart is a joyful heart. It is also a peaceful heart. It is not fighting self or others.

Forgiveness of each day's wrongs at the end of the day is the simple formula for joyful living. It works wonders in every relationship—between husband and wife—between parent and child—between you and the in-laws, the neighbors, the boss, and all other persons.

In the marriage relationship, true forgiveness means that you accept yourself and your mate as you are—a combination of virtues and defects. You cannot force your mate to change. You cannot change yourself a great deal. Conflicts still remain. But don't stack up hostilities day after day!

At the end of each day, clean the slate of all hostility and bitterness. "Don't let the sun go down on your anger." Confess. Forgive. Say these healing words: "Forgive me. I was wrong." Express your love for one another, just as God expresses His forgiving love toward you. Then conflicts and unhappiness have a miraculous way of fading into insignificance.

In the words of Dr. Karl Menninger: "Love is more

powerful than hate"; it "cancels out hate as water puts out fire." When you truly forgive, you forget.

It's easier to forgive if the partner indicates he is sorry and sincerely intends to act differently. But what if he continues in his wrongdoing?

As long as you don't forgive unconditionally, the other person will need to defend himself, so he will continue in his wrong behavior. Only your forgiveness will release him from the need to vindicate himself. This is true in any type of relationship. The more intimate the relationship, the more essential is forgiveness. In the closeness of the marriage relationship, we discover we live every moment by the forgiveness of others.

When a wife discovers the many reasons she needs forgiveness, then she will forgive. Doctor Gibson Winter, author of *Love and Conflict*, believes that a wife can realize that her own unresponsiveness contributes to her husband's unfaithfulness. "She sees her own need for forgiveness as she forgives."

Forgiveness is the only way you can love the one whose faults and weaknesses you've discovered.

Julie's closest friends, even her own family, can't understand her acceptance of her alcoholic husband. But Julie senses her own failures and weaknesses. "Who am I to judge him?" she questions. "He has many good qualities. This is his weakness. I have my own."

In other words, Julie forgives him his faults. When husband and wife are bound together in forgiveness, they can speak the truth in love.

Forgiveness doesn't change the past, but it certainly alters the future. It looks ahead. It sees future experiences to be shared. It anticipates lessons that need to be learned. Forgiveness doesn't keep a person down and tramp over him. It helps him onward and upward. Forgiveness gives a person a new page on which to write his life.

Forgiveness in marriage is not only confined to a case

of unfaithfulness. It is needed in every difficult situation—
for thoughtless and unkind words and actions as well as
for misunderstandings.

Doctor Winter claims that forgiveness is really "the
daily bread of married life. Forgiveness is the fabric of all
human life together."

Someone has said that when there is a continual harp-
ing on any mistake, on any misdeed or act of disobedience, there is no forgiveness. Forgiveness is forgetting
and not referring to it again.

When the children were small, I was brought up short
one time by an incident. One day a neighbor boy came
running into the house while I was scrubbing the floor.
He quickly apologized. I replied, "That's okay," and proceeded to mop up his dirty tracks. Then, like a bolt of
lightning, it flashed through my mind, *If that had been
one of my boys, I'd have scolded him!* I would have
remembered the many times I had reminded him not to
come in when I'm scrubbing. In other words, in remembering, I had not forgiven!

Forgiveness brings mercy and gratitude to the of-
fender. This is truly what love is made of. It comes from
the heart.

We ask for forgiveness. We also forgive. This is how
children learn to forgive each other. They learn through
visual aid.

A mother asks, "Can I force my child to say, 'I'm
sorry'?"

I personally believe a mother can tell her child that he
should be sorry for some wrong deed. But she should not
force him on the spot to say so. She can say, "Go to your
room until you can tell your brother, 'I'm sorry. Please
forgive me.'" But the decision is his.

Forgiveness is so very important in all family relationships—those of parent to parent, child to child, and parent
to child. Forgiveness is essential not only in the toddler,

in the spilling-milk and muddy-track ages, but also throughout the years. However, many parents find it especially difficult to forgive the teenager or the older child who doesn't accept their way of life.

Forgiveness is necessary whether or not the other person asks to be forgiven. True forgiveness is an attitude, a way of life.

Although Tim turned to drugs, his parents did not reject him. Every night they turned on the porch light for him. They welcomed his friends. All the while, Tim became more miserable. One afternoon at a buddy's house he fixed a potion of LSD, pills, and Cokes which he thought would be his final trip. To his amazement, he didn't die. As he stumbled toward home, after midnight, trying to hold on to his throbbing head, he met a former friend from the church. The boy placed his arm around Tim and told him how he could enjoy life with Jesus.

Tim believed. Right there on the spot he asked God to forgive him. Immediately a Presence, a cleanness, swept over him.

He walked home, carefree, lighthearted, happy as a lark. The porch light was on. He snapped it off and went to his room. His mother walked in unexpectedly.

Tim smiled and said, "Mom, I'm a new Tim. Jesus cleaned me up tonight."

His mother hugged him—smelly, dirty hair, filthy clothes and all—kissed him repeatedly, and cried through her tears, "Thank God, my boy!"

Forgiveness is the only way to family love and happiness. Try it.

Forgiveness is a command. God says we should forgive. Then He'll forgive us. Furthermore, we can't expect our prayers to be answered if we harbor ill will, resentment, or revenge.

The best example of forgiveness is Jesus Christ. While hanging on the cross, suffering, innocent of any wrong,

He said, "Father, forgive them; for they know not what they do" (Luke 23:34 RSV).

Another important aspect of forgiveness is to forgive yourself, regardless of what you've done or said. Chalk it up to your humanity. Learn from your mistake. Ask God's forgiveness. "If we confess our sins, he is faithful and just to forgive us our sins, and to cleanse us from all unrighteousness" (1 John 1:9 KJV). When we experience God's forgiveness, then we can truly forgive, voluntarily, repeatedly, and without reservation.

Forgiveness brings peace of heart to the individual and harmony to the home.

16
Good Parent-Child Communication

When family is important to parents, they put themselves totally into doing their best, into developing harmony and peace. This approach wards off many unnecessary conflicts.

Parents want to pass their values on to their children. To do so requires good communication between them. A good relationship is the key. Relationships, more than words, teach a child character and worth; although, of course, the right kind of words is important in communication.

The parents' words should show appreciation and love. They'll avoid automatic criticism and comments that create resentment and hostility on the part of the child. Some resentment creators to avoid are threats, accusations, sarcasm, name-calling, bossing, and bullying.

Words show that parents understand. Understanding is

communicated on the first day of a child's life. When
parents respond to the infant's cries, they show understanding. They are sensitive to his emotional needs as well
as his physical needs. They express love and acceptance
by meeting his needs, by cuddling and rocking, by hold-
ing him close, by their gentle and loving tones, words, and
touch, and by their talk. This begins the process of good
communication which continues through every stage—
from those early years on to adulthood.

An atmosphere of understanding and positive communication creates a good climate in which to learn. For
a parent to question when a child looks sad, "What's the
long face for?" only turns the child off. One shows understanding by statements such as, "Something unpleasant
has happened."

When a parent shows understanding, he can very
quickly win the child over. He then wants to share what
has happened. This holds true also if he hesitates or
refuses when asked to do a chore or to carry out a regular
assignment. An attempt to understand his unwillingness
to do it frees him to do it. There may be times when you
need to force him, but let that be the exception rather
than the rule.

Good communication requires positive listening—listening with sensitivity. The uninterested parent forces
the child to conclude that his ideas are unimportant. In
contrast, when Dad and Mom listen, the child believes his
ideas are worthwhile. He senses respect, which, in turn,
helps develop self-respect and a sense of worth.

Good communication early in the day sets the tone for
the entire day. A mother should be sympathetic to the
child who finds it difficult to get up, and not show anger
or scorn. She can identify with the child's feelings by
saying, "It is hard to get up this morning," or "It's so nice
to be in bed." Such statements create an atmosphere of

warmth and understanding. To scold and call him lazy produces a cold, stormy atmosphere.

Parents can avoid that before-school bedlam by allowing sufficient time. A child resents being rushed. The wise mother sees to it that the child gets sufficient sleep by getting to bed on time. Then he doesn't have to be hurried every minute. Very often when a child is told to hurry he'll resist the command by slowing down.

He should be given realistic time limits. Tell him that the bus comes in ten minutes. This is good for other times, also. When he is playing, tell him when the meal will be served and how much time he has.

A child's day may be spoiled when parents are overly concerned about his clothes. He should not have to worry about keeping his clothes clean. Allow him the freedom to run, play ball, or jump without concern for neatness. A child's clothes *will* soil. Inexpensive changes of clothing are so much better than daily sermons on cleanliness.

Breakfast is neither for long conversations nor for teaching polite manners or discipline. The family may be rather sleepy or grouchy. To try a pleasant conversation could end up in quite the opposite. Breakfast should be a time that the child enjoys.

Often a child may forget something as he rushes off to meet the bus. The best approach is to pick up the missing item and hand it to him. The statement "Here is your book" is more helpful than to say, "I've never seen anyone so absentminded. You'd forget your own head if it weren't fastened."

Give the child a few positive words as you part, such as, "Have a good day," or "God bless you today." These expressions are better than a reminder, "Don't get into trouble," or "Obey the teacher." As to the time he comes home, it's best to say, "I'll see you at 3:30," rather than a command not to be late.

At the end of the school day it's best for Mother or the

mother substitute to be there, to greet the child with enthusiasm and understanding, and be ready to listen to his/her news items. The child soon clams up if the first words are, "Don't throw your book on the chair," or "Hang up your coat."

Authorities tell us that this homecoming is one of the crucial times in a child's day. Surveys reveal that a large number of children fear coming home to an empty house.

Jan says she prepares a special snack, such as milk and cookies, and sits down with the children when they come home. Each takes a turn in sharing about his or her day, mother included.

I realize there are those times when a mother cannot be at home when the child returns. She should clear this before the child leaves in the morning. If that's not possible, then she should be careful to leave a note or a taped message telling where she is and when she'll be home.

When Father comes home is also important. Some fathers prefer a few minutes to compose themselves. However, for others, their greatest delight is to play with the children and hear about their day. If they don't get this opportunity to share, at the supper table is a good place for conversation.

Parents can make a time that's eagerly anticipated. Small children need Father or Mother to tuck them in. This time can be used for story time, for sharing what's on their hearts, or perhaps for reading Bible stories. When this happens, children look forward to bedtime. Some older children like to be tucked in, too. They shouldn't be laughed at or criticized because of it.

Sometimes parents need to leave the child. When this is necessary, the parents should be honest and not be deceptive. They should make adequate provisions for the child's care, but not run off secretly. The child may resent their going. Even though he cries, they can sympathize with him. They can say they are aware of his wishes, but that they are going to the party, dinner meeting, concert, etc., and assure him they'll return.

In difficult situations when a child has done wrong, a parent should first state his own feelings and thoughts without attacking the child's personality and dignity. They need to separate the child from the act.

When Johnny spills the milk, to say, "Stupid! You're always making a mess," attacks his personality. It is destructive criticism. However, the statement "I see the milk spilled. I'm sorry that happened. Here's a cloth to wipe it up," lets him know how you feel, but he doesn't feel attacked as a person. This is constructive criticism— omitting negative remarks. It communicates to the child that he is more important than the wasted milk or broken glass. Dorothy Law Nolte has stated, "If a child lives with criticism, he learns to condemn."

Good communication doesn't include threats. A warning serves as a challenge to the child and causes him to repeat his misdemeanor. He proves to himself and to others that he isn't a sissy.

There is an effective way of handling misbehavior without threats. If Johnny hits his baby brother, Mother can say, "Don't hit the baby. Hit the beanbag chair." If he hits the baby again, make him go to his room for a period. Johnny learns the consequences of his actions without any damage to his selfhood. Furthermore, too many parents forget about their threats. A child then loses confidence in his parents' words.

Using bribes is poor communication. Promising rewards for good behavior may be harmful to continued efforts. Bribes drive the child to undesirable behavior in order to qualify for a reward. Such reasoning conditions him to make stronger demands. Rewards are more helpful and more enjoyable when he receives them as a surprise. Then they represent recognition and appreciation.

The kind of questions some parents ask makes the child defensive and drives him to lie. If a parent discovers a broken toy the child has hidden, he should not cross-examine him. Naturally, the child will not reveal what he's already secretly hidden.

In such a discovery the parent should come out honestly and tell what he has discovered, perhaps making a comment that it's too bad the toy didn't last longer. With such an approach, a child learns that the parent understands. He can tell him his troubles. No doubt the child will also try to be more careful. Parents need to be examples in honest behavior.

Good manners, politeness, and social skills are largely learned from the parents' examples. Teaching politeness impolitely is hardly the way. Parents need to lead out in saying "good-bye" and "thank you" and "please."

When a child interrupts adult conversation, the parent should not angrily tell him it's impolite to interrupt. A statement to the effect that he would like to finish his story and then the child can speak is sufficient.

Good communication from parent to child includes praise. But praise his efforts and achievements rather than his personality attributes. Tell him he did a good job, not that he's a good boy. If you tell him he's a good boy, he may remember the thoughts he had about the parent that weren't so good; what was meant as praise will only serve to condemn.

A child needs to be made to feel that he can do something good. If he does a difficult task well, tell him so. Sincere praise for some job well completed, or even well attempted, enables him to develop self-acceptance and form a positive opinion of himself, of others, and of the world around him.

Dorothy Law Nolte has also stated, "If a child lives with praise, he learns to appreciate." This is so true. That's no doubt one reason that God advises us to be filled with praise—in everything.

Uncontrolled anger results in negative communication. Anger is an emotion which usually arises suddenly and unexpectedly. It's a part of being human. But we need to learn to handle it. When we lose our tempers we say and do things to our children that we never imagined possible. We resolve we'll never get angry again! Then something happens, and, quick as a flash, we lash out at the child.

It is possible to prepare ourselves in times of peace and calmness for times of frustration. We do it as we acknowledge the truth that children will sometimes make us angry and that it is possible to express angry feelings without attacking the child's personality or character.

The parent can identify his feelings by saying that he feels angry or annoyed. For example, when the child neglects to hang up his clothes, say, "I get angry when I see your clothes spread all over the floor. I feel like throwing them out the window." Such expressions allow us to get rid of anger. It's done without violence or severe punishment. To identify the feeling and express it verbally brings release.

At the same time, the child is learning how to deal with anger. The parents have given an example of getting rid of anger in acceptable ways.

The Bible warns us to "be angry and sin not." For those times when anger does get out of hand, and we say and do those things we're ashamed of, we need to ask the child's (and God's) forgiveness. Jesus Christ's power can help us control our anger so we don't use abusive or destructive words and actions. He can also teach us ways of helpful praise and criticism of our child.

Is discipline a means of communication? It certainly is. Discipline means teaching. We teach a child, "This is right—that is wrong." In those early years it's done mostly by example and by helping him obey.

Parents limit and restrict, to be sure, but they first identify the child's wishes and feelings. Then, without anger, they redirect them to acceptable actions. This leads to self-discipline. The child establishes inner standards for self-control as he identifies with the parents and their values.

It's how we go about stating limits that makes the children either accept or reject them. Parents must be sure of their convictions. It's important to clearly state the unacceptable conduct and an acceptable substitute.

It's very important for parents to state limits in a way which doesn't challenge the child's self-respect. For example, to say, "No TV until your lessons are done," arouses less resentment than to say, "You know you can't watch it now."

A child obeys more willingly when you repeat the limit than when you warn him he'd better stop what he's doing. When a child goes beyond a limit, the parent should firmly but kindly repeat the limit, without a lecture giving all the reasons. Take the young child by the hand and kindly guide him to do what you stated he should do. Actions speak louder than words.

The parents and the child involved may arrive at a solution, as in Terry's case: He came home an hour later than the set time. The following morning, his dad found that the car had a broken headlight, and there was a beer can in the glove compartment. The parents listened to Terry's story. He had gotten with a group which had access to illegal beer, and he'd gone along with them because he didn't want to be a "square." Terry's father stated that apparently they had a problem. The three of them together then agreed that Terry's weekend activities should be limited. At first he wasn't too pleased, but later he admitted he didn't want to belong to the group. He volunteered to pay the car damage.

Adolescents and teenagers usually react angrily when

parents set limits. However, inwardly they respect parents who do this and who are firm in their decisions, yet who listen and treat them as people.

Parents who spank their youngsters for every little act are not correcting the child but merely giving vent to their feelings. This soon means absolutely nothing to the child. However, I believe an occasional spanking, after repeated acts of disobedience, is very effective for the over-two-year-old child.

The Bible says, "Don't fail to correct your children; discipline won't hurt them! They won't die if you use a stick on them! Punishment will keep them out of hell" (Proverbs 23:13,14 LB).

Just a caution: there must be many hours of calm, kind, and gentle teaching, good relationships, and much showing by example, or punishment is not effective.

Good communication which has developed in the child's growing years continues through adolescence, teenage, and young adulthood. The child may be uncommunicative for a period, but parents need to do their part.

Love is the best communicator. With love, respect, and acceptance, parents and child will once again find close communication and relate to each other in harmony.

17
Fun Times Together

A child learns easily and quickly when he is happy.

A pleasant, enjoyable home atmosphere is conducive to developing "whole" children.

An unknown author gives this recipe for a happy home:

A Happy Home Recipe

4 cups love	5 spoons hope
2 cups loyalty	2 spoons tenderness
3 cups forgiveness	1 pint faith
1 cup friendship	Work and play
1 cup kindness	4 cups laughter

Take love and loyalty, mix thoroughly with faith. Blend it with tenderness, kindness, and understanding. Gently stir in forgiveness. Add friendship and hope. Season heavily with work and play. Sprinkle abundantly with laughter. Bake it with sunshine. Serve daily with generous helpings. This recipe serves any size family.

Note the generous amount of laughter included in this recipe. A sense of humor is important.

No one wants to be laughed at, but you can see the funny side of a situation while keeping a straight face—such as seeing your kindergartner all dressed for school, sitting on the table spreading butter on patent-leather shoes to make them shine!

Marion Leach Jacobsen, author of *How to Keep Your Family Together and Still Have Fun,* believes that a family needs "a strong, happy sense of togetherness." She is convinced that family fun, laughter, and recreation together are some of the parent's best tools for building family togetherness so essential to every member.

When fifteen hundred schoolchildren were asked what makes a happy family, the most frequent answer was "doing things together."

Do you enjoy your family—or do you only see the problems, difficulties, illnesses, uncooperativeness (just to name a few), instead of joys, rewards, and blessings? Seeing only the endless tasks and conflicts is a major cause of families falling apart.

Your children can be a great pleasure to you. This requires that you learn to enjoy them while they are small. The moms and dads who are too busy earning money and acquiring things, or too preoccupied in their own interests, or trying to keep everything tidy and efficient, have little time or heart for the children's interests. They're so busy they miss the real fun of watching the youngsters grow up through their many interesting stages.

One mother shared her regrets after her children were grown. Although they seem well adjusted to life, she asks herself if perhaps they could have been much happier if she hadn't worried about sneezes and had joined them running in the rain and been more enthusiastic about their imaginative play. Would it have been better if she had been less concerned about a well-balanced diet and occasionally enjoyed a lunch of jelly roll and soda pop or ice cream with the family? Should she have been less concerned about dirty hands and torn clothes and seen only the eagerness as they told about a wonderful adventure?

The mother concluded, "How I wish I had been less serious and more joyful. Children are tough. Health rules and cleanliness are only a part of life, but the one essential is a joyful spirit and laughter."

Family fun helps erase the resentments lingering in the children's minds from having to do a certain chore, or from when they felt misunderstood or got a "bad deal." I can't explain how, but the largeness of a child's mind enables him to recall the fun and happy times at home instead of the unpleasantries. Laughter and fun is the grease that keeps the wheels of family living running smoothly!

Family fun also depends on good parent-child relationships. A child's lack of respect for parents, or a disobedient, defying attitude can break up the best-planned family good times.

If parents can't control the children when playing games as they travel, or when playing table games, or when trimming the Christmas tree, there won't be much fun during these times together.

Playing with a child creates a very tangible closeness. It helps break down walls that keep parents and children apart. These walls may be discipline or parents' bigger size, strength, and knowledge.

That closeness is so important in the teen years. A mother who couldn't communicate with her teenager asked a psychiatrist how to get close to him. The answer was, "It's too late. Getting close to your son or daughter has to be done when the child is young." It is almost impossible to do if only begun during adolescence.

Building relationships is an important investment in future relationships. Ten or more years later it doesn't matter if you owned a dream house, or the latest gadgets, or attended every community and church activity. It will matter whether or not you took time to get close to your children through the family good times.

I think it's unfortunate that many fathers relegate this responsibility to the mother. Father is a special person. Mom is around all day and is taken for granted. In contrast, Father is gone most of the day in an exciting world. When he does come home and notices the family, they feel special.

Teenagers rate parents high when their father spends time with them. Most sons and daughters would gladly give up material advantages for experiencing acceptance and enjoyment by their fathers and mothers.

Family fun doesn't come easily. It takes some money. It is costly in effort and in time.

Many parents aren't home enough to have fun times with the family. In our modern culture, at-home times together need to be planned or the family will never get together.

Some family fun is impromptu and spontaneous. But the best family recreational program is one that has taken some thought and careful planning. Think together what your family would enjoy and can do.

Children do need direction in their play. They should learn creative play. However, there's one caution—children's play should not be overdirected. Parents should supply the materials for the children's play, encourage their use, then leave it up to the children how they'll be used. This allows for the children's own progress and development of creativity.

However, directing the child's play is no substitute for playing with him. When did you last play with your children? I don't mean direct their play, but actually play with them. Try it. You'll have a good time together.

Family fun requires a bit of mess and disorder in the home. If the house must be in perfect order, neither your children nor their friends will want to be there.

A living room has to be appropriate for such play. If you don't have a recreation room, it's really unwise to furnish your living room with delicate colors and materials.

One family was upset when the mother bought a new rug for the living room. They no longer could relax at home. Prior to this purchase, the family enjoyed the room—snacking, sprawling on the floor with books or toys, even scuffling with each other in a relaxed mood. Mother seemed to forget that she could clean or repair a carpet.

I'm not saying that children should have the run of the house. Not at all. But you need to allow space and time for family fun together. You also need to help them care for their things. Patiently teach them how and when. They may seem irresponsible, but mature performance comes eventually.

The day comes all too soon when you can keep your

house in order. (I'm experiencing that now after thirty years. It does seem soon!) You'll do your best to keep your home in respectable condition, but don't let that rob you of fun with your children.

You'll discover fun and delight in having your teen-ager's friends in your home, too. This will happen only if the children have enjoyed home and if their friends have been welcome through the years.

Special occasions and holidays hold a large place in childhood memories. Many adults recall Christmas as out-standing. For others, it's birthday celebrations. They need not be elaborate parties but a day when the child is the center of attention. It's his day, and very important to him. Other holidays that are fun days for many families are Halloween, Valentine's Day, and, of course, Thanks-giving Day.

Planning ahead and planning together as a family is half the fun. Somehow eager anticipation is greater than reali-zation.

There's so much of routine and work in daily family living, so it's essential that you take time to enjoy the family at home. Enjoy them while you have them with you to enjoy. Laugh together, not only in special fun ac-tivities but also as you and the other family members perform routine chores, eat, and play games.

There's much that tears a family apart in today's cul-ture. For your child to feel secure, to have trust, confi-dence, and faith, you need to help him feel close to you and to enjoy today. A faith and trust in Christ helps you develop a happy atmosphere. His joy and peace become a part of your daily living.

Enjoying each other in the varied daily relationships creates harmony in the home.

18
The Dignity of Work

"The daily grind of hard work gives a man a polish" is a saying we've frequently heard.

Paraphrased it could read, "The daily routine home-making chores give a woman strength of character," or yet this, "The daily responsibilities give a child a sense of worth."

We might as well accept work and enjoy it, for no one can go through life without work unless there is an abnormality. Attitudes count. Some work is drudgery, that's true. But we've got to do it. One's attitude makes the difference.

I've discovered that the day-by-day work necessary in family living can be a source of tension and frustration among family members. However, when parents and children have proper attitudes toward work, and together develop workable daily schedules, family chores can be done in peace and harmony.

Work is no disgrace. It can be rewarding and challenging. There's no substitute for honest labor.

Work is valuable—not only for the pay and benefits but most of all for work itself. It can lead to stability, personal development, and human satisfaction.

It seems that when Father Adam severed honest relationships with God, God decided that man needed to work "by the sweat of his brow" to earn a living. Work isn't necessarily a burden or a punishment. It's for man's own good. It's a gift.

Work is healing. After the death of her husband, Joyce took up practical nursing, which she had dropped at the time of her marriage. She says keeping busy diverts her mind from her sorrow.

Physical work can be therapy. It's good for emotional health. My husband is a college professor, at the same time studying toward a doctor's degree. It's good therapy for him to work in his garden—and, as a result, the family enjoys delicious strawberries and raspberries as well as sweet corn and other fresh vegetables.

Work is a blessing in disguise. This includes all types of jobs and daily work. There is a place for physical work.

I agree with Helen Wilshimer in this poem from the *Log:*

I've Often Found

I've often found that working with my hands
Has eased my heart when I have been distressed;
Despair has yielded to a straight, white hem,
A sock to mend, a crumpled gown I've pressed.
And once or twice when hope was strangely lost
The hurt was lessened when I baked a pie,
And I felt gayer when I washed the towels
In crisp, bright suds and hung them out to dry.
There is a rhythm of relief, dear God,
In quiet toil, and so I ask of You
That when life brings me disappointment, grief,
My hands may find some humble task to do.

Richard Starnes, a columnist, once wrote: "Kids need to work, and they need to work hard, for the good of their bodies and their souls. The creative joy of honest toil is a blessing. . . . A horse that stands idle in a stall will turn ornery and remain so until he is de-edged by work."

As much as we desire leisure, too much of it is dangerous. Doctor Charlie W. Shedd, author of *Promises to Peter,* believes that the most unhappy person on the youth scene today is the "full-time noncontributor." Although he boasts that he's doing his own thing, and believes he has arrived, it's not really where he says it is. He's not happy. Neither are his parents. Life doesn't owe anyone a living. Although there are days when we wish we could rest all day, that's not the way to achievement. Work done well is a chief source of self-worth and self-esteem. Living without responsibility in luxury, leisure, and ease is a dangerous way of life.

Parents should accept responsibility to teach children the dignity of work, so they can work effectively and enjoy it. This isn't easy. According to Dr. Shedd, it requires "careful planning, lots of discussion and a definite program."

There's more to it than pay. Motivation for work is not only to purchase our necessities but also to be able to give to those who lack.

Children need to be assigned daily chores according to age and ability and should only be allowed to skip them in an emergency. They can accept routine daily chores, such as making one's bed, picking up clothes, dishwashing, helping with meals, and caring for younger brothers and sisters, as a matter of course, without pay! It helps when parents make the weekly cleaning, ironing, lawn mowing, etc., as attractive and interesting as possible. Children catch Mom's and Dad's attitudes. When they're old enough, it's good to rotate the jobs on a weekly basis.

Daily chores remind a child that he's a responsible member of the family. Homework and music lessons are included as chores. The older child should help with administrative work—figure out how to get that new coat, plan the grocery list, check on machinery, schedule new jobs, etc.

In addition to at-home jobs, children should learn how to work for other people. This helps them learn to appreciate the difference in bosses. They learn to get along and to take orders. They learn to keep at the job and to understand people and situations—the way Dan did. He came home from helping a neighbor and explained, "I didn't charge anything. He's been in the hospital, you know."

Parents need to help children find challenges in their jobs and to take an interest in their work. A New York organization supervises young salesmen thirteen to sixteen years old. It reports that children with concerned parents show more responsibility than those left to themselves. Boys whose parents often took them to museums, art shows, and circuses were the ones who faithfully went their appointed job rounds. Those boys who were not involved with their parents and who were unexposed to the finer things, soon dropped out as salesmen. Also in the failure category were boys whose parents didn't know or didn't care about their son's job.

As much as possible, parents and children should work closely together in a cheerful spirit. This helps them to grow together and to think together. It gives a family security.

Work is important. Parents need to provide for the family, while at the same time teaching the children where money comes from, giving lessons on how to spend it wisely, even to save some, and how to share with others. But money should not be a consuming drive. It should not be the basis for what they do in life. As Christian parents, show your children that your chief vocation is to build the kingdom of God. Here, too, children catch parents' attitudes.

Leslie Paul, who made a social study of school dropouts in Britain, reports an interesting finding. The way a parent talks about his job in front of a child seriously affects the child's own work life.

He further states that a boy will have grave job problems if 1) his father takes a silent attitude toward his work, 2) if he has a resentful attitude and always complains about his daily drudgery, 3) if he has a purely mercenary, what's-in-it-for-me attitude.

Mr. Paul recommends that parents talk about the ups and downs with humor and tolerance. When a father hands down the rewards of his work to his family, his child will grow up to enjoy his own work.

The late R. G. Le Tourneau, a Christian industrialist, loved to work. He was still a busy man, serving God and people, after having made his millions. He believed that children need education. They need carefree, pleasurable hours. But we need to teach them the dignity of work and that accomplishments also bring pleasure. He felt that even compulsory work was better than idleness.

Sometimes parents have to "make" work and plan carefully. One city father resurfaced his driveway in an effort to give his son a summer job. Another family moved to the suburbs in order to have a small plot of land where the children could work.

Through the ages people have known work to be dignified and desirable for our happiness. As stated in the *Pentecostal Evangel,* "Work strengthens the body, sharpens the mind, disciplines the spirit. Jesus glorified work by spending years at a carpenter's bench."

Work is a blessing—a gift of God—an opportunity both for service to others and for self-improvement and enrichment of life. We can hardly improve on Paul's advice: ". . . study to be quiet, and to do your own business, and to work with your own hands . . ." (1 Thessalonians 4:11 KJV).

Family living requires work. That means everyone pitching in—accepting his share, enjoying it, realizing that he's a part of the team, and gradually becoming a responsible member of society.

This promotes harmony in the home.

Part 3

ORDER IN THE NATION

"If there is harmony in the home,
There will be order in the nation."

19
Living on Neighbor Street

The family that experiences harmony at home can reach out to others. Only from a secure home base where they can resolve their own conflicts and understand and care for each other, can they relate well to those in their community.

A smile, a listening ear, a helping hand, a cheery word are much in demand. It's in giving and in loving that one's own life is enriched.

Regardless of how much or how little interaction you have with your family today—regardless of your work schedule—you can be sensitive to what they are saying. You can sense the need for appreciation and love when Jack throws down his tennis racket and angrily criticizes his partner—when Sally bangs the door and isolates herself—when baby clings to you—when husband slinks in the chair—when parents are critical.

Hudson Taylor was quoted in *The Christian Leader's Golden Treasury* as having said, "A small circle of usefulness is not to be despised. A light which does not shine beautifully around the family table at home is not fit to rush . . . off to do a great service elsewhere."

Family is no island, although it is a separate unit of persons. Family exists in the midst of other families, in a neighborhood or community. Family members relate in one way or another to those various individuals living near them. People, not neat lawns and modern houses, make a nice neighborhood. It's what happens among families that counts.

Neighborhood is vanishing. Because of our mobility, we don't stay long enough to fix roots. Or aloofness may result because of selfishness. Many don't want to give of themselves, so they refuse to receive from others. They stay cool and keep their distance.

Bob and Tammy moved into a small town, and, just as they expected, the neighbors began to meddle. The evening they moved in, the elderly woman next door hustled over, introduced herself, gave them a fresh apple pie, and offered, "If there's anything we can do to help, just let us know." They thanked her cordially.

Several attempts were made by the elderly couple to become friendly, but Bob and Tammy stayed aloof—they weren't going to let snooping neighbors spoil their togetherness!

Two weeks later something happened which changed their minds. Bob was away on a business trip. Tammy locked herself out of the house. She asked the neighbors' help, but they couldn't get into the house, so she stayed with them. When Bob returned the next day, Tammy said, "I think they're great!" Bob quickly responded, "Let's be neighbors."

When do you think of your neighbors? Are they a nuisance? Do you care about them? How do you relate to them? Do you build fences?

Some people believe, as Robert Frost wrote, "Good fences make good neighbors." In other words, if they don't see each other there won't be problems.

There can also be invisible fences of indifference, unconcern, resentment, or hostility. To be good neighbors, we need to overcome these barriers. Perhaps the neighbor hides her hurts and needs. We can develop a greater sensitivity in order to detect unspoken hurts and needs. Along with learning sensitivity, we need to take time for others, to be available.

Abbey admits, "I know this lonely woman two doors from me. She corners me whenever she can. But I find myself dodging her. I just don't have time."

Rhonda indicates a similar feeling: "I'm too wrapped up in my own family and self, and all our interests. We never have enough time for what we want to do as a family!"

I can identify with Abbey and Rhonda. Our culture has programmed us to activity, to work hard to acquire more things. We're constantly pressured to *do* rather than to *be*. We're more comfortable *doing* through an organized group or *giving* to charitable causes rather than *being* that person who's aware of hurts and needs.

There may be times of intrusions, of interrupted plans, but there can develop communication and understanding between neighbors. One must keep priorities straight. Is life only for work, for projects, for activities—or is life relationships—caring—sharing—helping to meet other persons' needs?

The least of us can't say we aren't important or that we have nothing to give or to share if we have love in the heart. That's the key word to being neighbors, to becoming a neighborhood—love.

It's putting into practice God's commandment, "Love your neighbor as yourself" (Leviticus 19:18 RSV). Love is an act of the will—a commitment first to God and then to the other person. That person may even be an enemy—someone who doesn't like us.

A Harvard research revealed that Radcliffe and Harvard students who were former enemies "became friends, almost against their wills, when persuaded to exchange friendly, loving acts."

Alice had a similar experience. Her neighbor had spread a false rumor about her. She was jealous of Alice because her only child is deformed, and Alice has two healthy children. Alice said, "We used to be close friends. Now, I have no love for her. I avoid her like poison. But I know this isn't right. She needs a friend."

In spite of these feelings, Alice did want to be a friend. She did care. One day she prayed for God to give her love. Although some people accused her of being hypocritical, Alice began acting love—doing kind, loving deeds.

She began greeting her neighbor with a smile and a cheery hello. She shared her flowers and occasionally "needed" her neighbor to do a favor for her.

It wasn't long until Alice discovered her feelings had changed. No longer were her actions forced. She experienced a joy and satisfaction in these neighborly acts of kindness. She actually loved the neighbor.

You learn to love as you draw from God's unlimited source, and, like Him, you can't contain it. You pass it on.

Neighboring can be rewarding. There are always ways we can be neighborly and show that we care. Among your neighbors are there the lonely, those troubled and depressed, the ill, the aged, the unwanted? Show that you care by a friendly greeting, an invitation for a meal, by becoming acquainted with them and their interests. Put your love and concern into practical, helpful actions.

When you spot the moving van on your street, welcome the newcomers with a cold drink or hot coffee, or carry a casserole or pie over for their supper. We parents can help to create a feeling of neighborliness in our children.

Is it really asking too much to wear a friendly expression as you do your shopping—to allow the mother with the crying baby to go ahead of you in the grocery-store line—to offer your chair to an older person who comes into the dentist's office—to hold a door for the next person coming through?

Your neighbor has two small children, a tiny baby and a twenty-month-old who manages to get into everything!

For the last hour she's been trying to wash her windows, but the children are continually requiring her attention. You can tell she's getting frustrated. Can you help?

Gwen decided to bake a birthday cake for her neighbor—a busy mother who bakes cakes for her children's birthdays, but whose own birthday was just another day on the calendar. When Gwen took the cake over, the neighbor lady was coping with a sick, crying baby. It seemed life was too much for her. However, Gwen's cake changed that in a moment!

Ruth Ann says that when she steps outside to hang up the clothes, work in her flower bed, or to sit in the patio, the neighbor lady frequently comes out, too. Ruth Ann enjoys this opportunity for conversation and exchange of ideas. Sometimes she initiates the occasion to share when her neighbor is outside in her yard. During the winter months they may call each other on the telephone and say, "Come over for a cup of coffee."

Occasionally they care for each other's children when one mother goes shopping or unexpectedly needs to run an errand. Sometimes at play their children have their rifts and conflicts. The mothers try to understand what's happening and not take sides favoring their own children. They talk openly about their problems. They've also learned to forgive each other, and not hold a grudge or bitterness or resentment toward each other.

During the summer, they take turns helping the children plan activities and supervising them. They may go to the local playground, the library, the pool, drive to the country, or do some creative projects at home. This frees one mother for a week to concentrate on other activities or special work she needs to do. At times, the children are busy helping with family chores or are involved in other commitments and activities. Some of the children spend a week at camp.

The men of the neighborhood share their tools. Together they own a power mower, trimming shears, and a garden tractor. They plan their schedules ahead of time and know when their turns come.

Occasionally the neighbors eat together in a backyard picnic. They also share children's outgrown clothes rather than selling them at a garage sale.

Ruth Ann says, "It's good knowing someone is there —and we can share together, or listen, and know someone cares."

They give of themselves, as Edwin Markham's verse indicates:

> None goes his way alone,
> All that we send into the lives of others
> Comes back into our own.

One family I know plants extra rows of vegetables in their garden so they have some to give away. It's a point of contact with the family who's just moved into the neighborhood. It's a way to show love to the neighbor for just being there, or when there's a special need.

Susie says hers is one of three families who live in a suburban area and who share with each other. One family is an elderly couple whom the other two families have adopted as "grandparents." Each summer this couple plans a neighborhood get-together. They invite not only those families living nearby but also everyone who has lived in those same houses through the years. This couple sets the date for the potluck meal on a Sunday afternoon. Everyone appreciates this neighborly gesture.

In other areas, neighbors enjoy an annual picnic, ball game, or cookout.

Being neighbors usually involves children having fun times together—and sometimes there is a child searching for love.

Neighborhood children can pose conflicts and problems. How do you feel about the children playing together? Do you let your children run over to the neighbors' house any time they please?

Kay responds, "At our house we have set up certain guidelines. When my child asks to go to the neighbors' house to play, he must always ask the mother if it's okay to come. It may not suit her. It's always suitable for children!"

But how about when the neighbors don't have such a rule, and their children come to your house any time of the day, every day? Then what's your approach?

This calls for honest, tactful communication between the families involved in an attempt to arrive at a satisfactory solution. You need not apologize when plans don't allow them to come over, and you should feel free to suggest a suitable time. As a Christian neighbor, you should also talk to God about the situation and your honest feelings. Your main concern should be to show love and consideration, while at the same time honestly evaluating your own family's goals and needs.

Should the neighbor not cooperate and the children continue to come and go freely, then what? You can think of this as an opportunity to show God's kind of love. Take an interest in them. Give direction to their play. Occasionally play with them. Treat them as your own children and be frank about setting limits. When your children need to do a chore, or you have family plans, there should be no hesitancy in stating so.

Louise was frustrated at the frequent intrusions of the "neighborhood pest," whose working mother left her in the care of an older brother. He usually had other things to do.

After a number of summer days had passed, Louise could not forget the lonely girl's looks as she'd shoo her home. One day while Louise was praying, God seemed to tell her that the little girl was His child and that she needed love. Louise walked next door to the girl's home and invited her to come over. They'd find some games to play until Louise's own children awoke from their naps. She discovered that the girl was not a terror—just scared and lonely.

What would happen in your community and mine—not only in this generation but also in the next—if each of us who claim to know God and His love opened our heart and home to some lonely, neglected child in our neighborhood?

A loving neighbor is not snoopy, or a gossip, or one who makes the neighbor's business her own. Rather, she takes the initiative in being friendly. She may encourage her husband and family to initiate a neighborhood picnic as Orpha did.

Orpha and her family planned carefully. They would have a wiener roast and hamburger fry in their backyard. Each family would bring enough for its own use. Orpha would supply paper plates, cups, and the drinks. The children soon caught the excitement. They made simple invitations and personally delivered them.

The evening turned into one of fun and getting acquainted with some neighbors they had not known before. It became an annual affair—with the families taking turns at hosting the picnic.

A caring neighbor is concerned about neighborhood appearance. Rachel was in the yard picking up the sticks the wind blew off the trees. The neighbor children watched for a few moments, asked a few questions, and soon raced back to their yard and began picking up trash.

One homemaker planted flowers in a window box. The neighbors liked the new look. Soon the entire block was full of window-box flowers.

It's easy to show love to the one who's lovable and interested in you, isn't it? But how about the unlovable one—the one who turns you off—the one whose life-style and values clash with yours—the one in trouble? One homemaker pleaded the case of neighbors who had received an eviction notice because illness had kept them from earning.

The Jesus way is loving the unlovable, loving the one who needs help—and needs it immediately. You may shrink back from that assignment. "What! Me get involved in that accident (or fight, or drug case, or eviction notice)? They might sue me for interference!"

Attorney Neil L. Chayet says that is misplaced fear. After many years of careful research, he hasn't discovered any records of insurance claims settled in court or out of court against a "good Samaritan" who helped out in an emergency.

The family who loves and cares for each other will share their love and tenderness at all times. God seems to come through in difficult situations.

A positive, loving approach to neighboring resolves most conflicts and helps to avoid many others. This promotes order in the community.

20
Building Bridges of Friendship

Becoming friends with those of your community helps create order in the community.

A mother was enrolling her six-year-old son in kindergarten. The teacher brought out her records and began to ask questions:

"Does the boy have any older brothers?"

"No."

"Younger brothers?"

"No."
"Older sisters?"
"No."
"Younger sisters?"
"No."

At this point, the lad, who had grown increasingly unhappy and self-conscious, put in a wistful word. "But," he said defensively, "I've got friends."

> God knew we needed something more
>   Than budding earth and sunlit sky.
> And so He sent us friends to love,
>   To lift our hearts and spirits high. . . .

AUTHOR UNKNOWN

Friends are treasures. They bring a dimension to life that nothing else can bring.

The need for friends is universal—the human heart is the same in every community, the world over, as Landor has stated: "In hours of distress and misery, the eyes of every mortal man turn to friendship; in the hour of gladness and enthusiasm, what is our want? It is friendship."

Someone else has said "Building friendships is important to survival. The problem of friendship is the problem of life itself. He who has learned to love—and only he—has learned to live."

As we experience the hurts of life and respond to them positively, we become more sensitive to those in need. Through them we get in touch with ourselves, with life, and with God.

Debbie says, "I was absorbed in my own life and the family until we moved to a distant city. Now I take the initiative and make new friends. I know how it feels to not have friends. I need friendship."

The Bible says that one purpose God has in bringing us comfort is so we in turn can comfort others. We can share ourselves, our love, and our God with others. You can take the initiative and build bridges of friendship in your community.

Doctor Arlene Sitler, a social-science professor, related a project in one community. It was called Operation Friendship. Two families were matched together—a welfare family and a family of better means, with comparable age children. These families would share picnics, games, and fun times as well as hobbies and work projects, and sometimes just fellowshiping together in each other's homes.

In one instance, a child who had been totally unpresentable, and who lacked interest in school, began to come to school clean and presentable. She took a real interest in her classes.

It was not so much that food, clothing, and material goods were being given but the fact that another family was caring and sharing. Knowing that someone cared gave a new lease on life to the girl and her whole family. The Source of such love is God, because "God is love."

In another community, through a local school committee, mature mothers go into homes of underprivileged persons. They gain the mother's friendship and gradually share how to keep house, how to prepare nutritional foods and keep within her income, how to clean floors, and how to clean and mend clothes. In some instances they teach her how to play with and relate lovingly to her baby and preschoolers.

In some homes there previously were predelinquent children in grades 4-7. After six months of these services, the children's behavior at school changed noticeably. They became interested in life, in themselves, in their studies, and in others.

One teacher-mother, Vera Casey of Berkeley, California, initiated a project where professionals as well as volunteers relate to unwed mothers and help them learn how to care for their children.

Bridges of friendship—that's what this old world needs! Bridges from your house to mine and on to other parts in our communities.

Friendship consists of forgetting what you give, but gratefully remembering what you receive. It's becoming interested in others, not trying to get others interested in you.

To be able to help build bridges of friendship in your community, you need to begin a friendship with one person.

Friendship is kindness, an inner goodness.

Friendship is the company loneliness desires.

Friendship is wisdom.

Friendship is the "gladness of selfless giving."

"Friendship is sweetness, that makes life worth living."

Sometimes I fall short of being such a friend—do you? But there is a Friend who possesses all these qualities all the time! He never changes. The Friend of all friends—who sticks closer than a brother—is Jesus Christ.

Make Him your friend. Allow Him to help you build bridges of friendship in your community.

21
Of One Blood

Order in the nation will never exist as long as prejudice and hate exist in communities. Too frequently an accent, unusual facial features, or different color of skin have become high walls separating families and neighbors.

A child isn't born with hate in his heart. Who is it, then, who teaches him to despise and fear, or to respect as his equal, a member of another race or nationality? Is it his playmates—his teachers—parents—radio or comics? Probably it's not any one in totality, but all of these determine his attitudes and how he expresses them.

What can we do about this serious problem of racial tensions? We must strengthen our laws, but while legislation may take away segregation it cannot take away prejudice. As Billy Graham so aptly states: "It will never be solved until it is solved in the hearts of the people."

We must first open our minds to the fact that we are all equal in God's sight. We can also begin listening and opening ourselves up in small groups and learn to know each other better. As someone has stated, "Prejudice is the child of ignorance."

It also becomes an important part of the parents' job to help their children resolve the resentments, prejudice, and hate they may be tempted to feel. I believe that we parents hold the key which opens our child's heart either to accept or to reject other peoples.

The child above three years of age has already absorbed your feelings, whether or not you have verbalized them. He is learning how prejudice acts, or how people act who are not prejudiced.

Parents must possess a genuine interest in and love for others. I repeat, it must be the pure stuff. Forced politeness won't cover a heart's attitude. The latter will easily be detected by the child through your daily remarks, through your reactions, or even through voice tone as occasions arise involving other races.

When our children were young we opened our home for two weeks to a boy and girl from Brooklyn, New York. They were Puerto Rican. On one occasion the two youngsters and I were in a group. It so happened that after the youngsters left the room, a mother, a total stranger, edged her way to me and inquired, "Are they causing you any trouble?" For a split second, I looked at her questioningly, because I had completely forgotten the difference in our nationalities. Then I caught what she meant and with honesty and sincerity I answered, "No, ma'am, we've had absolutely no problem with them. And if our children were to behave as properly and courteously away from home as Elba and Herman do, I'd be most happy."

With this mother was her twelve-year-old daughter. Without a doubt, she knew what her mother had implied.

Often parents speak convincingly of their love for the faraway Africans, the Chinese, and others—peoples they've never lived with. Yet, at the same time, they shun the migrant workers in their community, the blacks, or the new immigrants. Such love is a sham. It's false. True love covers all nationalities within our reach, just as the wings of a mother hen safely cover her brood.

For instance, one mother and father very faithfully remembered those faraway children who didn't know God's love. They prayed for them. They contributed to support missionaries in other nations.

One day their eight-year-old son related the accomplishments of a classmate. His enthusiasm ran high. He voiced his admiration—both for the boy and for his success. As he finished his account, the mother shrugged her shoulders and said, "Well, he's only a ————." The boy happened to be of another race.

Frequently parents encourage prejudice within the home, often unconsciously. They favor a more intelligent child, or the one who is quiet and creates little disturbance. Or perhaps they wanted a boy—and God gave them a girl. They don't totally accept her for who she is (or vice versa). Parents need to be fair and impartial and not play favorites.

I think ignorance is the greatest factor causing disrespect for other races. Too many parents depend on hearsay, or on newspaper propaganda. They do not stop to question whether the negative things they hear and read are actually true or false. Even Christian parents are too gullible on this score.

Another factor for nonacceptance of other races is not being acquainted. Few people, however, can use that as an excuse, as in many of our communities there are peoples of other nationalities who have moved in during these recent years.

Let's think now of some positive approaches to resolving prejudice. We need to remember that God is no respecter of persons. He sees no separate group or race. Through Jesus Christ, the walls are broken down, and His love can remove prejudice from anyone's heart. Right attitudes are so very important.

Parental attitudes are carried into community relationships. Parents can encourage their son or daughter to befriend the newcomer who may speak broken English, or to befriend the Vietnamese, the black, the Chicano, etc., at school.

There are ways to do this. A cousin of mine relates her experience as a child many years ago. Her family lived in a southern state where there were a number of Chicanos. The majority of the youngsters "picked on" them. My cousin's mother knew about it, and frequently she would fill my cousin's pockets and those of her brothers and sisters with roasted peanuts. They then shared these peanuts with the Chicanos.

What a lovely way of making peace!

Peacemaking for most of us is just this—relating to others in a positive way. It's avoiding conflicts. It's helping others to resolve their struggles and problems.

There are the war brides who have come to many different communities. There are immigrants, refugees in the large cities, migrant workers, Mexicans, and blacks. International students abound all over the States. Mission groups frequently send a representative to the homeland.

Invite the war bride and her husband into your home. Learn all you can about her country—main industries, customs, religion, the people. Don't do so in order to make fun of them or for comparison, but to increase your knowledge.

The same is true of the international students. Located across the land are agencies whose business it is to arrange weekend tours for such students. If possible invite a student into your home during the holiday season. Befriend the migrant, the unwanted one in your community. You may stimulate your church group to take up such a project.

Utilize the family discussions of national and community events to help your children understand other races. Assign them specific duties as you entertain or befriend these peoples.

It's interesting to me to note the many Bible stories involving various races. This is especially true in the New Testament. After Peter's vision of the "unclean" animals, when God told him to eat them, he was invited to the house of a Roman officer who wanted to know more about God. Peter, who had always believed the Gospel was only for the Jews, went to the house of Cornelius. God's presence and Spirit fell on the entire household, affirming the Gentiles as His children also (*see* Acts 11:1–18).

On another occasion, Christ commented concerning the faith of the woman of another nationality. He said hers was the greatest faith He had seen. These and many other incidents point up the fact that "God is no respecter of persons," that no one race is superior. The Bible says that God "hath made of one blood all nations of men for to dwell on all the face of the earth . . ." (Acts 17:26 KJV).

That is literally true, because science cannot distinguish race through the most minute examination of blood.

Blood types are the same in all races. Blood transfusions of similar types can be used successfully in different races.

Even the brain taken from a man's head does not identify him as to race. True, some races show differences in capacity. But anthropologists say that this is due to differences in training. Given an equal chance, "they show themselves to be very much the same in brainpower."

Several years ago at a major educational conference, the noted American lecturer Dr. John H. Furbay illustrated this truth so well. He is personally acquainted with—in fact, helped train—native personnel for the airlines in Ethiopia. The parents of these pilots live in the bush. They can neither read nor write. In a ten-year period these African pilots have had a 100 percent safety record. He challenged the same for any American airline.

As we parents accept other races; as we befriend the outcasts and the unwanted; as we "love our neighbors as ourselves," our children will catch the same spirit.

It is a sin to hate and disrespect each other. We are all brothers, of common origin, with similar innate capacities and intelligence, for we are "of one blood."

Remember:

> Regardless of color, race, or name,
> In the sight of God, we're all the same.

22
Respect for Authority

We need law and order just as much as we need justice, liberty, and equal rights.

I agree with Mr. Ramsey Clark, a former Attorney General of the United States, who said "The long history of mankind tells us you can have neither justice nor order if you don't have both." I also add that you can't have order if respect for authority is lacking. Lack of respect and lawlessness go hand in hand.

Our nation is made up of millions of homes, very small but forceful units. When law and order and respect for parents are taught in the home, children will carry these same principles outside their home and will respect school and civil authority.

Let me illustrate: Walter was a high-school junior and president of his class. One of his teachers was inefficient and very uninteresting. The pupils made fun of her, contradicted her, and finally rebelled. One day they started a general riot, and the teacher fled to the principal's office. The principal then sent notices to the parents of the students to come to school.

Walter had not participated in the rebellion. However, at his request his father came to this meeting of the principal, teacher, parents, and children.

The parents were very vocal in taking the children's part and justifying the children for rebelling against an inadequate teacher. Finally Walter asked permission to speak. He stood until all were quiet and then said, "Fellow students, we have been in the wrong. We showed lack of respect for our teacher and refused to try to cooperate with her. We as a class are guilty of doing wrong. We rebelled against our teacher. Whether our cause was just or not, we were in the wrong, and I feel we should apologize to our principal and to our teacher."

When Walter sat down, the principal said with emotion, "I want it understood that Walter was not involved with this disrespect and rebellion, but he identified with his fellow students as their president. If all students were like Walter, we would not have this problem."

Immediately the atmosphere in the room changed. The parents and students quieted, hostility faded, and the students voted to apologize and try to work with the teacher.

Not only did Walter lead the way to a satisfactory solution to the problem but he also gained in prestige with his fellow students. They told him afterward that they knew he had done the right thing—but they had built up this trouble to their parents and didn't want to back down.

This is an example of what happens when respect for authority is taught in the home. I am personally acquainted with this family, and I know respect was "caught" in this home as Walter's mother and father respected each other, respected the children, and respected and obeyed civil and church authorities.

The Bible tells us very clearly that God has set up those in authority to protect people, to bring about justice, to punish the evildoer, and to encourage those who do well (*see* 1 Peter 2:13–15). This is necessary if a nation wishes to survive and progress.

It's impossible for everybody always to do exactly as he or she pleases. It's difficult for me to understand why many insist on breaking the laws, on being disrespectful of officers, participating in destructive demonstrations, and engaging in constant criticism of the government. At the same time, they want to live in a safe and progressive society with the protection of civil authorities.

Someone retorts, "But how else can we bring about change?"

I agree that there are many social changes necessary. However, we can and should voice our opinions and criticisms to the proper authorities and through legitimate channels. It is never right to break laws in order to (hopefully) bring about other laws—even though the latter are for justice. The Bible says, "Shall we do evil that good may come? God forbid!" (*see* Romans 6:1).

We can't expect more from our youth than we adults are willing to do. What if you don't like the president of the country? To be sure, you can't change the election results. It is not likely that any demonstration of hostility or disappointment will change the situation. So let's think together of your responsibility to those who are in power, who control the country, even though you disagree with some of their policies.

No doubt there are times when a wife doesn't agree with her husband, yet she appreciates the areas where they do agree. She continues to show consideration, kindness, and to love and respect him. There come times when even though she disagrees she cooperates with his wishes for the sake of the family. She does not hold these differences of opinion against him. She doesn't build up resentments and hostility because of them. She hopes for this same kind of respect from her husband.

In the same way parents should respect the president, focus on his strength, and remain loyal to him. They influence the child and help him develop a proper attitude of respect for our leader—regardless of whether or not he was their choice.

Remember, attitudes are caught, not taught!

Some authorities believe that women hold the key to any social change! Because of our close relationship with our children in their formative years, and our influence in society, we can help initiate reforms.

An unrooted tree has many symptoms of disturbance. The leaves dry up. The blossoms wilt. The tree bears no fruit. If left alone, it will ultimately rot and decay. However, if a tree is properly rooted, signs of decay will disappear. This is also true of life or society.

Does our society show the symptoms of being rootless? Have we lost our sense of relationship—our roots—with God? One outgrowth of a close relationship with God is a respect for earthly authority. It's one way of demonstrating respect for Him.

In these rootless and troubled times when, among many other ills, law and order is laughed at, let's bring respect for leaders and authority back into our society, beginning in the home. From homes come persons, both young and old, who form our society.

It is true that those in authority who want respect should faithfully fulfill the duties which belong to their responsibilities. Having said this, however, I still believe that as an individual I cannot decide that I will respect and obey only the one I judge to be faithful in his assignment. God doesn't hold me responsible for others' actions and attitudes but for mine, and for being faithful to His truths.

Let's be interested in justice, in peace, in love, but let's use proper channels to voice our convictions. If authorities still ignore change, let's be careful not to instill hatred and disobedience in our children.

The Bible says God sets up the rulers. A Christian citizen follows the Word of God, which further says: "Every Christian ought to obey the civil authorities, for all legitimate authority is derived from God's authority, and the existing authority is appointed under God. To oppose authority then is to oppose God, and such opposition is bound to be punished" (Romans 13:1, 2).

Let's obey those in power and the laws they set up for our society and for our protection. Obedience is not only the safest action but it is also right. Obedience to authority is an example of obedience to God. There's one exception—should authorities make demands contrary to God's Word, then we will "obey . . . God rather than men" (Acts 5:29).

Above all, let's pray for our leaders. They have a difficult task to guide millions of people in our country. They have a tremendous responsibility. They make far-reaching decisions, often worldwide in scope.

According to Scripture: ". . . prayers, intercessions and thanksgivings should be made on behalf of all men: for kings and rulers in positions of responsibility, so that our common life may be lived in peace and quiet, with a proper sense of God and of our responsibility to him for what we do with our lives" (1 Timothy 2:1, 2).

Let's unite as adults to restore law and order and respect for our leaders, that we may help achieve order in the nation.

23
A Good Citizen

To maintain order in the nation, its citizens must appreciate the good in their country. They need to recognize what this good is, and realize the progress that has been made. We in America have many freedoms and conveniences to be thankful for.

I'm very much aware, too, of the evils in our society and of many wrongs in government. America is a Christian nation only to the extent that persons are Christian and act Christlike. At the same time, I firmly believe that the blessings and privileges we have today are a heritage from God Almighty. In recognition of this, we should express our gratitude and appreciation by being good citizens. Only as we follow and love Him can we continue to receive His blessings.

"Righteousness exalts a nation, but sin is a reproach to any people" (Proverbs 14:34 RSV).

I'm wondering, have you ever stopped to analyze just

why our nation has developed so much in just a few short centuries? Is it a mere coincidence that within 350 years' time a continent is as populated as ours and its natural resources are so greatly developed? Is it mere coincidence that a nation of such geographical proportions is connected from one extreme point to the other by paved highways? Is it just a happenstance that democracy exists—with its benefits of equal rights, hospitals, free schools, and churches?

Certainly this is not just luck.

Our country was founded and settled by many God-loving peoples who wanted only a place to call their own; a place to eat, sleep, and work; a place to rear their children; a place to worship their God according to the dictates of their conscience.

God made a difference in our country—not a super-race—not mere man-created achievements—not man's genius or ability. God promises, " '. . . for those who honor me I will honor . . .' " (1 Samuel 2:30 RSV). We are the recipients of His grace and mercy promised to our forefathers.

God endowed persons with wisdom and ability to explore and to discover the natural deposits of minerals, oils, and other raw materials. God gave the wisdom to men to discover His secrets of atoms, of scientific laws, of outer space, of biology, and of medical discoveries. Down through the centuries, since the beginning of time, God has endowed men with wisdom, skill, courage, and determination to uncover and use His creation.

It's God through man who has made possible the exhibitions of a century of progress—and, oh, if only we today would recognize and honor God as the Source of all wisdom, all knowledge, all achievement, and all courage!

Man studies. Man observes. Man experiments. Man earns money. Man governs. Man regulates. But who made him an intelligent being instead of a moron? Who gave him health, in contrast to being a paralytic? Who gave him wealth, as compared to the underprivileged worlds?

We sing: "Protect us by thy might, Great God, our King." And that's just what it will take—God's almighty power and not armies, missiles, or bombs—to protect us from an enemy and to ensure the continuance of our freedoms.

"Long may our land be bright With freedom's holy light," states a phrase from the song "America." What is this freedom? The freedom we enjoy doesn't give us license to do anything we want to do. Men crave freedom to do as they choose—yet this does not mean that there are no limits or restraints. There is no such thing as being free in general. Freedom is always freedom from something or freedom to do something. The Puritans found freedom to worship in America, but they gave up their freedom to buy many kinds of goods and enjoy comforts. They found freedom from the oppression of King James, but were not free from the Indian attacks.

Freedom is always a matter of choosing. You are free after breakfast to choose your task of ironing clothes or visiting with the neighbors. But after your choice is made, you have limited yourself by that choice and, in a sense, are no longer free.

Freedom also means restraint. You are free to drive your automobile on the highway. Yet if you and everyone else were to drive at any speed, anywhere, with no traffic rules or lights, your freedom would soon be taken from you.

Unless we restrain freedom in many ways, no one can enjoy freedom at all, because freedom involves other people. Anyone who thinks only of his own rights will probably feel that everyone else is obstinate or unreasonable.

As good citizens of this democratic freedom we realize

that freedom brings choice and restraints, and involves other people. And we realize, too, that state and national laws are for the good of all, not just to benefit one person.

Let's celebrate our gratitude with prayers of thanksgiving for our beloved country, which has been richly blessed of God.

Let's renew our desire to be good citizens, to respect and obey the laws of the land as long as they do not conflict with God's laws. Let's use our rights only to the point where the other person's begin.

Let's pay our taxes—grateful that we live in a land where we can own our own homes and businesses. In some lands the individual's possessions have all been taken away from him.

Let's enjoy our homes, our families, our communities, our schools, our churches, our democracy, and not be chronic gripers.

Let's use our freedoms to live as peaceful citizens, while at the same time expressing concern for those who may be in need or who are discriminated against. Let's do what we can to bring about change—and to bring about peace.

Above all, let's return to God, the Giver of our peace, liberty, and happiness—the One who waits to receive us when life is ended. For, after all, as enjoyable as life is, it is only transitory. We are only pilgrims and strangers passing through, looking for that country "whose builder and maker is God."

You see, life here serves only as a preparation for that life beyond, which never ends. Even now, we who love and serve Christ are citizens of that other country. So let's be successful ambassadors for our King and invite others to transfer their citizenship to the kingdom of God. Let's pray specifically for our national leaders and for all who are in responsible positions.

Remember: Only a sense of gratitude and appreciation will give you a desire to be a good citizen.

24
Youth Power

According to John Fischer, former editor of *Harper's* magazine, young people have four choices in today's world. He said, in *Minister's Tuesday,* that they can 1) *drop out* with the use of drugs, alcohol, sexual liberty, mystic cults, or mountain hideaways, or 2) *run away* to another state or country, hide in the woods, or revert to the soil, or 3) *revolt,* and overthrow the adult world. The final choice for youth is 4) *try to gradually change* society, "one clod at a time."

This latter is probably the most difficult. It isn't easy; nor is it a sensational, inviting way to go! But I recommend it as the best. In the long run, it pays the greatest dividends—personal satisfaction and a sense of fulfillment by making a positive contribution to society and oncoming generations. Thank God for these youth who are changing society "one clod at a time"!

Too often, we adults focus on the bad news about youth. However, surveys indicate that only a small minority are radical, delinquents, and extremists. It's time we became more interested in young people and in their interests. We need them—these creative, energetic youths.

Someone has said that the "government and institutions must conserve the past and present. The individual is creative. They must work together."

I admire youth's courage, bravery, determination, power, energy, and vision which can be channeled for good—for themselves and for others!

Several years ago Miami's teens, almost thirty thousand of them, conducted a decent rally. Excitement ran high. They shouted as they listened to famous entertainers presenting decent songs. They heard speeches on religion and on morality, and they were challenged to have a meaning and purpose to live.

In our community an estimated 800 persons joined in a community "Walk for Development." The majority were youth. There were also a few children. By evening, some 350 persons had completed the 25.8-mile route. One college senior with a broken leg walked over five miles on crutches!

Community individuals and businesses sponsored each participant, paying a specified amount for each mile he or she walked. Over ten thousand dollars was received. Forty-two percent was sent for a project in Haiti—building water lines for villages. Forty-three percent was designated for a local camp for low-income children and for a community counseling service. The remaining 15 percent was given to the community development fund.

The participants decided where to channel the funds. One student voiced the feelings of each one involved: "It gave me a real sense of personal accomplishment."

We're proud of what the youth of a private Virginia college did several years ago. The college was promised a government grant for their much-needed library if they could raise an equal amount of money. But the money didn't come in. The date for the grant was running out.

Then the students stepped in, determined to raise the necessary funds. They decided to have an auction. With confidence, trust, and prayers for God's help, they got to work.

They pooled all their creative ideas and resources. Some designed Christmas cards. Some made candles. Others baked cakes, cookies, pies, rolls, and doughnuts. They contacted community women for donations. Some called back home to parents, to neighbors, to friends, and to businessmen, asking for pledges. One student contributed the money he had saved for a motorcycle. A girl

donated the five hundred dollars her grandmother was
going to give her as a graduation present. The surround-
ing community and faculty homes were scoured for arti-
cles which could be sold at the auction. With the help of
these dedicated youth, the need was met and the library
soon became a reality.

A number of students from this same college are also
involved in social projects. One such project is the Satur-
day Adoption Program. Children from underprivileged
areas are bussed into a central meeting place and each
interested student selects a child. The boy or girl then
relates to this student during the entire year.

They provide the child with learning and social experiences previously unknown—such as supervised play with
other children, spending a dollar in town, cooking and
baking together, tutoring, etc.

In every community, youth are in action. One community organization prepares one hot meal daily and teens
deliver the meals to senior citizens at home, frequently
helping the aged person to feed himself or herself. At the
same time they talk, sharing of local and personal news,
thus helping to bring a bit of cheer and hope.

In local communities teens excel in tennis, swimming,
softball, and basketball. Others are involved in sewing or
in agriculture and farm pursuits. Some participate in
choral groups, in the local band, or in piano playing.

A hot-rod club in California helped fight a terrible forest fire, supplied food for needy families, did yard work
for the elderly, and cleared cemeteries as part of their
daily record of community service.

In one year, a Boy Scout troop in Michigan contributed
10,500 work hours to such conservation projects as hand
planting 57,000 pine trees, installing 1,400 trail markers,
and building 307 birdhouses and feeders.

A YMCA Junior Leaders club revived a nearly dormant

Y and increased its membership from 250 to 1,700 in an area in great need of recreational activities.

Some one hundred Madison, Wisconsin, ninth-graders became lumbermen and carpenters one summer. They joined a city-school forest project, which included the cutting of 15,000 board feet of lumber at the 267-acre school-district forest near Verona, Wisconsin.

The youngsters marked trees, cut them, skidded them to a portable sawmill, and used the lumber to build a 24-by-48-foot shelter, a 32-by-16-foot building, two toilets, and four 32-by-16-foot tent frames.

Many young people help in their local church activities; others serve abroad.

Some teen teams travel across the United States organizing Youth for Christ groups and encouraging already existing groups. Some go to other countries.

Bible clubs are teen-directed in many high schools. Groups plan, prepare, and participate in Bible-quiz programs at annual conventions. Some years ago a team of barefooted, bluegrass country kids won the Youth for Christ quiz championship. This team represented towns varying from those with no population listed to one of one thousand people. Yet because of years of hard work, sacrifice, and drill, they carried off the honors.

One young person conceived the idea of distributing literature in a house-to-house canvas of 2.5 million Detroiters. He had a vision, plus experience. He previously had joined two thousand European and American teenagers who crossed the continent of Europe giving out or selling three hundred tons of Gospel literature in three months.

With the loyal cooperation of many other young people and organizations, the city was covered house-to-house in ten days' time.

My own church denomination sponsors Voluntary Service—a one- or two-year, six-month, or even a summer assignment. Hundreds of youth serve in hospitals, children's camps, camps for migrants, camps for handicapped, in orphanages, in communities, among the neglected, underprivileged, and minority groups; and abroad they serve in hospitals, or as teachers, and in reconstruction and agricultural projects.

High-school students in Charlottesville, Virginia, helped a classmate, Johnny, who was severely injured in a car accident and faced with huge medical and hospital expenses. Classes were dismissed for one day to allow the students to raise money for his expenses. They sold baked goods, washed cars, delivered doughnuts from door to door, collected bottles, and offered services for household jobs.

The senior class sponsored a dinner and a baseball game. They also gave up their traditional class trip. They persuaded the local radio station to stage a five-hour radiothon for community persons to call in and state their contributions. A student went immediately to the donor's home to collect the gift. All the money went to help pay Johnny's bills.

Youth can have wholesome recreation if we adults help them. One hot-rod group, called the "Jehus," drive carefully, not furiously. They also tear apart and rebuild cars. They take special pride in helping motorists stranded by flat tires or mechanical breakdowns. They stress courteous, safe highway driving.

A Los Angeles radio station and a local retailer sponsor a "teenage underground" to promote music other than rock 'n' roll. The organization offers members albums of classical music and concert tickets at special discounts, a key chain with a secret number, and a membership card.

It's not a gag to convert anyone, nor is it to knock other products, but it's to encourage youngsters who prefer this type of music. "More than seven hundred applied for membership in the initial mail response to the offer," reported one of the disc jockeys in charge of the project.

One group sponsored a local teenage beauty contest in which participants were fully dressed! They were tired of the accepted philosophy that a beauty queen had to appear almost naked in order to be judged. Yes, there were plenty of contestants—enthusiastic ones, too.

Youth love adventure. Adventure, let me remind you, is not to destroy or abandon old directions but "to invest them with new dimensions—with new learning, new promise, new hope." That's what's happened in the new Jesus movement among youth. A *Time* reporter congratulates their sincerity and their enthusiasm. They have put new life into Christiantity. It's a "startling development," he says, "for a generation that has been constantly accused of . . . copping out with sex, drugs and violence."

These young people have an air of love, hope, joy, and unselfishness about them. They experience a different quality of daily living because of Jesus' power and presence. Former drug addicts, criminals, delinquents, advocates of free love and situational ethics, now live by the Ten Commandments. They follow Jesus' teaching of unselfish living and a concern for others.

The adult world had better think twice. Before we criticize today's youth, let's remember we've pretty largely made the world they're living in! We're largely responsible for having shaped their character.

One authority laments that youth's rebellion and undesirable behavior is directly related to our modern industrial living. According to him, so many working mothers have "robbed the family of its inner adhesiveness and authority." Security, acceptance, and faith—the child's most valuable assets, the most stabilizing factors—are missing.

On the other hand, when parents are examples of the "good life," when parents praise their good actions, when parents become interested in them, youth respond accordingly. The majority of youth uphold their parents' beliefs, though they may express them in different ways.

I'm challenged and enthusiastic with youth's power and potential. They will not be silent or inactive. The important thing is to channel their energy correctly, so that it doesn't erupt into violence.

If parents and the adult world do not harness this youth power for good, the young people will channel it in the way they want to—sometimes in ways that are not beneficial.

Young people need direction and challenge. They need right motivation and inner controls. Youth need something to do! Under the umbrella of right, truth, and good, youth accomplish great things!

At home we parents should heed the Italian proverb, "Praise youth and he will prosper." Yes, more praise needs to be given for what he does well, for his helpful gestures, for his accomplishments, however small. This, not excessive criticism, will direct him on the road to success and help him make his "ought" a "want to."

A columnist recently accused teenagers of having poor manners. One girl responded, "Since manners are supposed to be taught in the home, the blame lies with parents."

God holds us parents responsible to give right directives. The greatest challenge we can give our youth is love and loyalty to Jesus Christ. Then His power coupled with teen power can change your home, your community, and our nation!

Let's pledge ourselves, parents, to challenge and encourage youth, with God's help, to use their time, talents, energies, and minds to build up "one clod at a time"—not to destroy.

Youth can help bring order in our nation!

25
Help Prevent Crime

Crime is happening right next door almost daily. It's involving people we know and children who go to school with our children. It's no longer a city problem or a problem of the poor kids from the ghetto. It's also the problem of the suburbs and a problem of teenagers from well-to-do families.

Crime has now reached a national crisis, including many youngsters under the age of fifteen. Current reports are unpleasant. We don't like to hear such facts—and rightly so. Frankly, they make us quite fearful of the future, as well as fearful of people and places.

In recent years, we've all been shocked at the serious crimes of assassination of national leaders. We're shocked at the rising crime rate, which includes murder, rape, robbery, assault, shoplifting, etc.

Crime is a problem bigger than the newspaper headlines. Benjamin Fine, author of *1,000,000 Delinquents,* says, ". . . we must look beyond the front-page news . . . and ask ourselves one all-embracing question: Why did they do it? And then these questions: Where shall we place the blame? How shall we find the solutions? . . ."

J. Edgar Hoover, the late FBI director, believed that our rising crime rate is a "direct product of self-indulgence and irresponsibility"—a result of a permissive society.

A student suggests that young people are only following the examples of adults: . . "police taking graft . . . parents fixing parking tickets . . . heads of state cheating the government . . . friends smuggling perfume across the border."

Causes of today's crimes also include unemployment, rising prices, poor living conditions, and drug addiction. Some crimes are committed by career criminals—people who make a living at crime. There are authorities who blame parental cruelty, anger, frustration, boredom, and broken homes.

People commit crimes. People can also work at preventing crime. In a lawless age, parents don't need to panic. They don't need to blame the schools or friends. They can help prevent crime by providing a good home.

A good home need not be up to date with all the latest conveniences. The house isn't of primary importance. A good home is one where there is love—where the parents love each other and each child. There is unity—both parents are available and united in attitudes and discipline. They keep communication lines open.

A good home is a place where there is reasonable discipline. Bill, a twelve-year-old boy in a training school, had slashed the upholstery in a number of parked cars and scratched the paint. He did this in a fit of anger after he was beaten severely and unjustly by his father. Discipline such as this can be terribly damaging because it communicates rejection.

A good home is where parents are happy to be and give of themselves to their children and do not substitute material things for meaningful family relationships. In one study of homes which produced delinquent children, seven out of ten of the families failed to do things together that would lead to a sense of sharing—there was no family fun or work. Meals were seldom eaten together.

A good home is a place where God's laws are respected

and obeyed. Parents help prevent crime by being examples of what's right. The best way to teach honesty is to
be honest with your marriage partner, your children, and
those persons you deal with on the job. The best way to
teach discipline is to be a disciplined example before your
children. The best way to teach obedience is to be obedi-
ent. Parents teach respect for human life and property by
being respectful.

The old saying, "Actions speak louder than words," is
still true. It's what you are before your children at home
that really counts.

Keeping an extra dollar when a cashier gives you incor-
rect change, or helping yourself to an extra newspaper
without paying for it, may seem a little thing, but it's
teaching dishonesty.

Many of our criminals started by stealing little things
such as candy or groceries. When they got away with it,
they moved on to larger items such as radios and TVs.
Then they went on to commit more serious crimes such
as hijacking or bank robbing.

We do our children no favors when we overlook the
package of chewing gum they pick up in the supermarket,
or cover up for lies they tell. We do our children an injus-
tice if we cheat on our income tax so they can have a new
bicycle, or tell half-truths in order to get what we want.
Lying, disrespect, and unruliness often begin at home—if
not by example, then by lack of example.

Just as tragic as the parent who sets a bad example is
the parent who sets no example at all—the parent who
spends little time with the children, who leaves the teaching of values to the schoolteacher, the TV set, and the
other children in the neighborhood.

Too many lonely people today feel that no one cares
what they do, so they lash out in hurt and anger by defying social and moral restraints. As a parent, act out your
love. Place your attitudes in the perspective of Jesus—a

stance that says, "Treat other people the way you would like to be treated." Keep in touch with the world of your children. Only when you really want to hear and feel with the child can you communicate faith, values, attitudes, and convictions.

A sheriff from my community gives his feelings on the causes of crime and what parents can do:

> Well, we can blame this on the ghettoes. We can blame it on unemployment. But I think basically we go back to the home, the home environment. When people are not busy, this causes crime. Mothers are not home; fathers are not home; parents do not know where their children are. The kids have too much free time.
>
> Everyone used to farm. No one has chores to do now. They come home from school in the summer, and about the only thing they do is mow the grass or go to the pool. I don't have the answer, but I think this is the biggest problem—a breakdown in the home.
>
> Parents usually aren't interested until they have a problem like this in their home. Then they'll come in, and they'll want to do everything possible. Usually it's too late, but sometimes they can be helped.
>
> Kids need boundaries and want boundaries. I can take our children, for example. They'll come to me and say, "Dad, may I do this?" And even the way they ask, you know that they don't really want to do it. They want you to say "no." And I think if parents listen carefully to the tone of the voices, they can tell their children "no" and they'll go along with it, even though they'll give an argument sometimes. But they know it's for their own good.

The sheriff makes some very important points for parents, especially in light of the fact that almost one-half of the arrests made are of teenagers and young adults.

At the conclusion of an article about violence in schools in an issue of *U.S. News and World Report*, a Texas school official states: "Parents want more structure, and students do, too. There is always a minority that feels any rule is bad. But more and more are realizing the need—in school and in society—for rules."

Community leaders can cooperate in crime prevention and initiate positive programs. Several years ago, a newspaper article highlighted a most interesting experiment in the Arizona high schools. Four convicts spoke at special student assemblies. They revealed their own mistakes and urged the youngsters to benefit from them.

At the age of seventeen, Sam A., now serving a life sentence, helped two others kill a man during a robbery that netted only fifty cents. He said, "Now four lives are lost just because we didn't think twice. We didn't consider other people or their property. We thought only of ourselves."

Charles R. said he had no respect for authority. He got away with "small stuff"—candy bars and cookies, then hubcaps—and became overconfident. He advised, "The law never gets overconfident. The law always manages to get you in the end, and you wind up in prison like me."

Dave D. was a dropout and turned to robbery and burglary to support the drinking habit typical of his crowd. He told the students, "After a basketball game you're better off buying soap than a six-pack of beer. You might be saving yourself a lot of trouble later on."

Ronnie T. started using marijuana at ten years of age. He made a plea to his listeners: "Stop it now if you're taking marijuana, pep pills, or going on marijuana-beer kicks. Stay in school and get an education, because without it you'll turn to crime."

These convicts appearing in person and relating their stories greatly impressed the young people.

In Corpus Christi, Texas, an antipoverty program

aimed at teenagers has cut juvenile crime in half. Interestingly enough, it also has helped the 450 from better homes who worked without pay as teachers and recreation leaders. They have other interests than throwing "water-filled balloons at passing cars, crashing parties and joy riding in stolen cars." Furthermore, according to Sgt. C. B. Mauricio, in poor areas, the complaints against teenagers for vandalism, glue sniffing, petty thievery, and gang activities have almost ceased since the programs got under way. "In one area, we had to keep a police unit on duty full time to prevent gang fights. We don't any longer. The results are nothing short of fantastic," says Mauricio.

In addition to being an example, there are practical ways to prevent crime. Police officers urge people to use common sense by making it difficult for criminals to victimize them. Don't present easy opportunities for someone to commit a crime.

Never leave your keys in the car. Don't leave keys at parking lots or repair shops. Keys can be duplicated in a very short time.

When you park your car, lock it. Take the keys with you. Store any valuables in the trunk rather than in plain view inside the car. To resist nighttime vandalism, park in areas that are lighted.

It is also wise to lock your home when you leave. Close the garage door. Don't leave notes on the door in easy view telling where you've gone and when you will be back.

Store equipment such as lawn mowers, garden hoses, ladders, tools, or bicycles. don't leave them in your yard overnight or while you are away.

Update the locks on your doors when you change residences. If you should lose your keys or they are stolen, then, too, have your locks changed. Give a key to each person in the family who needs one, rather than hiding one outside in the mailbox, flowerpot, or under the door-mat.

Be careful whom you allow to enter your home—a locked door does little good if you open it and let a criminal in. Request that repairmen, salesmen, and solicitors show their credentials.

When you leave on vacation or go for a short trip, cancel all deliveries, such as milk or newspapers. Check to be sure that all doors and windows are locked, and leave a light on. Have a neighbor keep an eye on your place and check it periodically.

If someone does break into your home, report it immediately. Don't touch anything until the police arrive.

Be concerned about what happens in your neighborhood. Be willing to report suspicious activities. Support the legal process and exercise your voice in local affairs through your vote. Support adequate lighting. Be ready to work with others. Provide activities for the young people in your community. Be willing to support the local police. Most important, obey the law yourself.

Authorities are alarmed that today's parents seemingly don't have standards. Society seems to uphold a slippery morality. We need to remember that there are higher laws than society's laws. They are God's laws, which clearly define right and wrong.

Miss Genevieve Blatt, attorney and former Pennsylvania Director of Internal Affairs, recognizes godlessness as a basic cause of crime, and religion as a basic cure: "We were a God-fearing people at one time, and proud of it. We must be that again if we expect to see the crime rate substantially reduced."

I agree with Miss Blatt!

Let's not get panicky about crime. Let's do something about preventing it—now! Let's put God and His laws back into our daily living in our homes and communities!

Part 4

PEACE IN THE WORLD

"If there is order in the nation,
There will be peace in the world."

26
World Neighbors

Many people in our country live in alleyways.

I do not mean that their homes are crowded or that they are living in the street, but that their minds are cramped and literally pinched into a narrow mold of routine and mundane activity. Their breakfast never varies. It's always orange juice, coffee, and toast. They always shop at the same stores and always visit the same friends. They are not unhappy. They are satisfied and almost complacent. That is the shame of it.

We may not identify ourselves with them, but far too many of us have isolated ourselves in one small part of the world, blind to all the rest about us.

We sit at our breakfast tables and read in the paper that half the world goes to bed hungry each night. Then we reach for our third piece of toast. We know that thousands have lost all their possessions and are forced to go to a foreign land, but we add property to property. We know that millions have never heard the name of Jesus Christ, but we take going to church on Sunday for granted.

The world has become small through our transportation and communication systems. Its problems lie at our doorstep, and we cannot help but stumble over them. Billions of people are now our neighbors. We must expand the horizons of our interest and knowledge to live with these many peoples.

Once Jesus told a young lawyer that he must love his neighbor as much as he loved himself if he wished to have eternal life. But the lawyer realized what this might involve and so he asked, "Lord, who is my neighbor anyway?"

Jesus answered by telling him the story of the man who was attacked and beaten by robbers as he was traveling. After taking all his money and valuables, they left him lying half-dead by the road.

Very soon a priest chanced that way, but seeing the man, he crossed over to the other side of the road and hurried on.

A church officer came next. He pitied the poor beaten man and stopped to look at him. "The poor fellow's half dead," he murmured as he started on.

Finally an outcast happened by. When he saw the man, he stopped and went to him. After applying first aid, he took the man to an inn where he could stay until he was well. "Take good care of him," he urged the people in charge. "I'll bear the necessary expenses" (*see* Luke 10: 25–35).

It seems that the answer to the question "Who is my neighbor?" is answered by the words "The one in need."

Our neighbor, then, is anyone in need to whom we can go—and our going is almost unlimited. Our country is the world and each individual is our brother.

Our hearts and minds must be big and broad enough to enfold the world, but we must also be discerning enough not to overlook the individual who lives near to us.

You welcome the new family next door, the "foreigner" down the street. When your child comes home from play and laughs at the new boy or girl at school who talks so queer, you draw son or daughter close to you and explain that people in other cultures do have their own language, and to speak English clearly and fluently requires many years.

We can find many ways to relate to those around us, but how can one become a neighbor to someone far away in a country such as Formosa or Vietnam?

Sometimes families can go to strange and faraway places where they can meet needs, but most of us must stay where we are. In this case, we can bring the place to us. "But how?" you ask.

Well, let's say your family wishes to be a neighbor to a hungry family in Bangladesh. How can you bring India's neighbor into your home?

First, you can buy a large, colorful map and tack it on the wall in some conspicuous place. Then locate the areas of need in Bangladesh and mark them in red. Next, go to this library and ask your librarian to help you find books about the country which have colorful pictures and up-to-date information. Find some books written on the level of your children and spend some time as a family reading and studying them together.

You, as parents, or an older child can write to the president of a college nearby and ask for the name of a Bangladesh student enrolled in the school. Invite him or her to spend a weekend with you. Perhaps the student may want to model the native dress or cook an Indian-style dinner for the family.

Invite missionaries on furlough from Bangladesh into your home. They could give excellent information about the needs of the country and maybe help you learn a few simple expressions or phrases from one of the native dialects.

Pen pals are also fun. You and your children would enjoy corresponding with a Banglalesh family. Obtain names and addresses through your church's relief agency or through a national organization.

At Christmastime you would enjoy packing gift bundles for your neighbors in Bangladesh.

Maybe next year you will want to "adopt" another family of another country and learn to know them in the same way.

There are many reputable agencies who represent starving, homeless, and needy persons worldwide. No doubt your own church denomination supports groups in various other countries. You can contact one of these and acquaint yourself with current needs and possibilities.

You may wish to support (or "adopt" as some call it) an orphan, by contributing a specified amount monthly. Some couples have adopted war orphans.

You receive the news of floods, earthquakes, famines, and wars across the world. You can spread goodwill as you respond to these immediate needs by giving materials or by giving money. Or you may designate surplus grains for starving areas. Contact government leaders who make the decisions to help meet disaster needs—food, clothing, and medicine.

Perhaps you may be able to go in person to disaster areas to help in cleanup or distribution. If not, at least you can serve to promote peace and concern through sincere prayers.

Our world is changing rapidly. You must prepare your children for a new and different future. You can do this by helping them to accept and become acquainted with world neighbors. This is easy when you remember that we are all children of God—in Him we have one Father.

In the Old Testament we read, "Have we not all one father? hath not one God created us?" (Malachi 2:10 KJV).

If God is the Father of all peoples, then beyond nationality, race, creed, and social and economic differences, we are all brothers. Just as God cares about the suffering of each of His children, we must feel concern about the hardships of our brothers and sisters at home and around the world. There is a poem in my book *Heart to Heart Poetry Album* which expresses my feelings:

Your Neighbor

Who is your neighbor? He whom you
    May find afar or near,
Whose aching heart or worried brow
    Your helping hand may cheer.

Your neighbor? He—the crippled, blind,
    Neglected, homeless, too,
Awaiting words of faith and hope
    From such a friend as you.

Your neighbor? He—(because his skin
    Is quite another shade)
Disowned, mistreated, shunned by man,
    Though by your Father made.

Your neighbor? No wall can divide
    'Twixt color, race, or creed,
For Jesus clearly said to all,
    "He is the one in need."

27
War and Peace

Sons, husbands, and fathers enjoy home, comfort, happiness, and a good life. Suddenly they're taken away from family, friends, and familiar surroundings in response to the call to war.

In one of my travels, I sat beside a young GI returning to duty from a ten-day furlough with home folks, now on his way to the war zone. He was hesitant and fearful—leaving a young bride, loved parents, brothers and sisters at home.

It's so difficult to understand why there has to be war. It's hard to accept!

Is there peace for those who go—for those who stay?
I share several letters from my files:

> Our son's homecoming would have been in April.
> But last fall he was killed in combat. We miss him so.
> Do you have anything to encourage me, his mother,
> and my family? We did learn from his buddy that he
> found Christ before he died.

In the second letter a mother relates her son's "calling"
and determination to be in the air force:

> My son had a dream. He wanted to go in the service
> and fly. He read all he could on the subject and talked
> and dreamed. . . . He wanted two years of college,
> because he thought he would have a chance to ad-
> vance faster. We thought college would keep him from
> getting killed. Were we wrong to try and protect our
> only child?
>
> Then he entered the hospital for an operation . . .
> he is still in pain . . . and can't get his strength back.
> . . . Now he has withdrawn from college and plans to
> go in the service. He can't get the service off his
> mind. . . .
>
> We're confused along with him. Pray that he won't
> lose his faith.

Another letter is very brief. It is from a mother request-
ing prayer for her oldest son who is going overseas.

The family members are bewildered and frequently
frustrated. Wives, sons, and daughters feel abandoned
and lonely. Parents' hearts are torn and sad over giving
up a son in a war that seems so unnecessary and endless.

One mother found comfort and courage in God, as
quoted in *Our Daily Bread:*

I Cannot Go With You, My Boy

Son, I must leave you in God's hand;
I cannot shield you from war that's planned by man,
I cannot hold your hand in mine in air, on sea, and land,
I cannot dry the tears that fall,
I cannot fill that aching void,
I cannot fill the lonely hours;
    But God can!
I can but wait, and pray and trust.

BONNIE MCREE

It's very difficult for the soldier, too. He undergoes many traumatic and shattering experiences. He's snatched away suddenly from all he's known and loved, into a life of war, hatred, and brutality, and often vice, drugs, and crime. He has time hanging on his hands. He is forced to be on his own—to make decisions or to unquestioningly follow orders. Either, or both, for him may be totally new territory.

His ideas and beliefs are tested to the limit. Before going he may not have had time for God, but as one veteran soldier commented, "No fellow can be in a foxhole and deny that there is a God."

A young husband and father came home gladly. His wife eagerly awaited him. They enjoyed many of the same things as before. But he was very silent, often evasive. He frequently had a faraway look. He didn't enjoy the many social whirls with their friends.

The young man even suggested attending church on Sunday, but his wife thought it ridiculous and refused to go. For several weeks he consented. Finally he told her, "Honey, if you want to stay at home, okay, but I've got to go to church and worship God. I found Him on the front lines. His presence meant everything to me. I promised if He brought me home again, to you and the baby, I'd love Him always. I can't go back on Him now."

During his army days, a GI in Asia, Frank Vogt, wrote about his experience. He had chosen to believe what others had told him—that God didn't exist. But one night when he saw God's sky from a shell-hole, he realized that he had been deceived. Now—he felt so near to God and admitted that he had been alienated from Him. It was incredible to think that he had to come to this "hellish place" in order to find God. He wished that he had known Him before. This encounter moved him to tears as he asked God to be his friend. He concludes with, "Strange, since I met You I'm not scared to die."

Isn't it tragic that young men haven't found God before such shattering experiences? If parents and churches would bring Christ to them and to all men everywhere, maybe there would be no war. That's a dream. We await the day when "swords will be made into plowshares" (*see* Micah 4:3).

Meanwhile wars continue. Men leave. Some return. They need our help as they readjust to life at home.

As the veterans reenter the civilian community, they have many new and difficult adjustments. Many who are still eligible will take advantage of the liberalized GI bill and enter school. Others will have no problem finding jobs. Still others will have difficulty. Perhaps the most difficult adjustment will be a social one—can they relate to those around them? Will their family and friends accept them?

Some families, community groups, and churches help plan for the young men to adjust and reenter regular life. Those relating to the men need to welcome them with deeds and words of love. They need an openness. They need to be friendly, unshockable, understanding, and patient.

This is especially true of the immediate family—wife and children, or parents, brothers, and sisters. New and completely different relationships begin now between the ex-soldier and the other family members. He's not the same person as when he went. He can't be. He has endured hardship and fatigue. He may have scars of combat, remembering fear and watching men die. He'll never forget these experiences.

The returning GI is usually more mature. He remembers the hours, days, and nights of aching loneliness. It will be difficult to match in civilian life the excitement, adventure, and danger of those years in service. It may be difficult for him to settle down. He has seen human nature at extremes—at its best and at its worst. He has faced the severest of all temptations. He may have been pressured into actions totally against his better nature.

This is a picture of the ex-soldier. He's a different person from the one you knew before he went. What is your approach to him? How do you help him in his new life of peace and not hate?

I have adapted J. Gordon Chamberlain's suggestions, from his book *The Church and Demobilization,* as to what you can do:

Treat him as a person of worth, and basically normal. He is not an invalid. Should he be injured, still treat him naturally.

Let him decide to talk or to keep silent about his experiences.

Create an atmosphere in which he'll want to take up his favorite sport or hobby and return to normal social life and work. He doesn't need anyone to push him.

He needs patience, love, acceptance, and, above all, to see your faith in God and in him.

>   Be a good listener and take time to get reac-
> quainted.
>   Be open to receive a new person. He has done a
> lot of living in totally different situations from the
> ones you have lived in.

What he doesn't need is a "foxhole" at home, or another
battlefield. He needs to discover life anew, which is possible only as one relates in a daily personal way to Jesus
Christ.

Although many sons, husbands, and fathers choose to
serve in times of war, others do not. They register as
conscientious objectors and give several years of alternate
service in some constructive work. Some resist the draft
and accept the penalty.

I want to share a bit about the alternate choice as conscientious objector. I praise God for a government which
allows this kind of choice. It is legal. It is honorable. It is
worthwhile. It is building up rather than tearing down.
It is peacemaking rather than hate-making.

Any man who feels called to be at peace with himself
and His God can register his convictions. The local draft
board gives him the corresponding classification. He then
contacts the appropriate agency, which assigns him to a
job that is available.

As a peaceful approach to war, the young men give two
years in some positive, constructive labors. They may be
assigned to work at hospitals, mental institutions, orphan
or retirement homes, or community services, both rural
and inner city. Others go overseas to underdeveloped
countries and help in hospitals, agricultural development,
etc.

Many young men have chosen this alternate route,
among which were two of our sons. John served in Mexico
in agricultural development. Martin chose an assignment
in Bolivia.

For two years Martin related to agriculture and community development. He first learned the language. Then, with another young man, he went to live in an isolated area. Their home was a rustic, ten-by-fourteen-foot structure—large enough for bunk beds, a chair, a stove, and a small cupboard. They cooked their own meals. They planted and harvested crops, using fertilizer. They raised pigs and rabbits in an effort to demonstrate more productive methods to the native people.

They helped form entertainment such as ball games and crafts for the community youth. They were available for emergencies. When heavy rains flooded out hundreds of families, they helped evacuate the people, helped administer shots against fever and other epidemics, and helped distribute food sent by relief agencies.

Martin remained an extra year to help a group composed of several religious denominations initiate a colonization program in cooperation with the Bolivian government.

Thousands of Indians born in the same high mountain areas of their ancestors are forced to leave for lack of land. At the same time, Bolivia possesses thousands of acres of jungles. The government is making this jungle area available to the Indians. But first they must clear the trees and underbrush, build a shelter, and learn how to live in a totally different world!

Martin and a group of other young folks help them become oriented to a new life-style as they adjust from a cold mountain climate to a hot, humid, semitropical climate. They must learn how to dress appropriately, how to plant gardens and crops, how to eat totally different foods from their former diet, how to prepare and preserve the corn, beans, squash, etc.

These helpers also minister to the Indians' physical, emotional, and spiritual needs. They teach hygiene and child care. They also conduct Bible classes. Most of all, they take time to sit and listen, to eat with the natives and to interact with them in work and fun.

Is there peace in time of war? There can be for the individual who, regardless of where he or she is, finds the Giver of peace—God.

Let's be peacemakers in our time—not war makers.

Part 5

THE INDIVIDUAL IS PEACEMAKER

28

A Peacemaker Is . . .

I admire statesmen who negotiate peace between nations, the negotiators between strikers and employers, the judges or other professionals who settle disputes between husband and wife, between parent and child, or between neighbors.

We honor such men as Dr. Martin Luther King, who use peaceful methods to bring minority groups into proper relationships with other groups within a nation. However, without a doubt, the unsung peacemakers are those many individuals who in day-by-day living "seek peace and pursue it," as the Apostle Peter advises (1 Peter 3:11 RSV).

In my previous chapters I've already shared ways of avoiding conflicts, and means by which conflicts can be resolved. Flashing into my mind now are other peacemaking incidents involving persons who are at peace with life. I wish to also include these in this book.

A friend of mine relates an incident involving a friend of his who was deer hunting. He had gone out early in the morning and taken his stand. He'd braved the cold and patiently waited for a deer to come within range. Then he sighted it. Quickly he cocked his gun and shot. He saw the deer fall. He hurriedly ran to claim his prize. Just as he stopped by the deer, a man stepped from behind a thick bush and said, "Hey, what do you think you're doing taking my deer?"

The amazed friend replied, "But, I shot him."

The other man advanced a few steps and roughly responded, "Liar! I shot it!" and began to curse and swear.

This friend stepped back, stating quietly, "I know that buck is mine. But it's not worth a fight or angry feelings. You can take it." And he walked off.

A peacemaker goes the "second mile" to insure harmonious relations. He/she may accept wrong rather than retaliate or demand rights.

In the early years of our nation's life, a farmer noticed that the corn in his corncrib was disappearing faster than he was using it. He was concerned, but didn't know what was happening. One night he decided to hide in the crib and see if he could discover what was going on. Shortly after midnight, he heard the door being opened slowly and cautiously. A lantern appeared, and his neighbor stepped into the corncrib. He was carrying some empty sacks which he began filling with corn.

The owner waited for a while, then stepped out from the darkness and politely spoke: "That's difficult for you to do alone. I'll hold the sack while you pour." The amazed culprit could only cooperate.

After the sacks were filled, the owner helped the man carry them to a waiting wagon down the lane.

He never lost any more corn.

"Returning good for evil" (*see* Luke 6:27 LB) is a valid road for a peacemaker. Jesus indicated that in so doing you "heap coals of fire on his head" (Proverbs 25:21 RSV). In other words, your kindness and love make it "hot" for the other person. He/she can't stand the pressure and is uncomfortable in your presence. Your actions burn within him. He recognizes his wrong, and under the Holy Spirit's leading he comes to terms with himself. Before long he'll respond in love and kindness, too.

In my local city of Harrisonburg, Virginia, a terrific

peacemaking happening occurred some years ago. It was just prior to the siege of racial violence in our cities.

A group of concerned persons formed a human-relations committee. Included were pastors, several college professors, and some interested community persons. They personally approached local organizations and shared their concern with authorities involved, deploring the segregation in the hospital, bus terminal, and school system. They contacted restaurant owners who refused to admit blacks, and businesses that wouldn't hire black persons. They shared with city officials their unhappiness with the housing conditions of the blacks.

The committee shared with church and community groups. They got together a panel representing various racial groups who also appeared in church and community groups upon invitation.

Slowly the restaurants opened their doors to blacks. The hospital dissolved its "black floor." A segregated school for blacks was dissolved as such, and black children entered the other city schools. Merchants hired black employees. The city built adequate housing to care for those of lower income.

As a result, our city was unscathed during those months of burning and ransacking of white areas by blacks from other cities, although attempts were made. One night a local black girl walking to her home was stopped by two well-dressed men driving a luxury car with an out-of-state license plate. They offered her a large sum of money if she would gather her people together and create trouble. She refused, saying, "We aren't interested." The following morning she related the incident to a white friend whom she worked beside at a factory.

Another time, a busload of blacks from a large city drove in one night to set fire to a newly developed shop-

ping center near the black community. (The shopping
center had been built after the evacuation of many of the
blacks from their former homes.) This plan, too, was
thwarted when the local black community wouldn't allow
the arsonists to proceed.

I recently read in the *National Observer* of Myrtle Rob-
inson, a seventy-year-old widow in Washington State. As
hobbies, she baked cinnamon rolls and communicated
with long-haul truckers through her citizen's band radio.

One day over the airwaves she invited a friend to taste
her freshly baked rolls. Her good deed seemingly ended
in a tragedy. The invited guest, plus the uninvited ones,
created a traffic jam and clogged the trailer park where
Myrtle lived. Her landlord promptly evicted her. Immediately her truckdriver friends started a fund drive
which helped her relocate in another trailer park.

God's creative Spirit of love can unite with your spirit
at any time and help you sense those needs around you.
It doesn't have to be something big, something that receives public sanction and notice, or something that is
initiated by an organization. Those are all important and
recognized methods of helping; but, you need to respond
to what your heart tells you to do, and what is natural for
you.

I'm reminded of the words spoken by our Lord, "She
hath done what she could" (Mark 14:8 KJV). The incident
took place just prior to His Crucifixion. Influenced by His
teaching, a terribly mixed-up woman had been changed
into one who "got it all together." This beautiful woman
then spent all her savings on a bottle of fragrant ointment
which, in an act of total sincerity, devotion, and love, she
poured over Jesus' head.

The onlookers protested, "What a foolish thing to do!
She should have used that money to help the poor."

But Jesus' response was, "Hey, quit your griping! Let

her alone! She's showing her appreciation in her own way. It means everything to Me, as I face My death."

She did what she could. That's all that's required of you and me. I'm so glad for that!

Peacemakers don't just happen. They are persons interested in other persons. They respond to others because they care. If necessary, they are willing to risk themselves, their reputations, and their security for the sake of misunderstood, rejected, or neglected persons.

A peacemaker is one who cares.

29
Blessed Are the Peacemakers

"Peace, peace!" is the popular cry everywhere.

I think that most of us, in our desperate desire to bring about peace in the world, are at a loss to know what to do. Perhaps we can get direction from this comment: "Hard to dislike a chap who likes you, isn't it? Well, there's your peace plan."

The peacemaker begins on a personal level. You pass it on. Someone helps bring about peace between two clashing people. They turn around and help resolve conflict in someone else's life. "Pass it on. It's the Jesus thing to do."

Peace is established as a person is transformed from within, and not through building external structure. Unless one's attitudes, goals, and desires change, no laws or systems will be adequate protection.

Fighting, quarrels, and strife begin in the human heart—the heart that is jealous, envious, hostile, resentful, and full of guilt and hate. You and I must get down to the causes of racial strife, poverty, civil wars, world wars, and family strife.

The person who is at peace with self isn't fighting others. You are confident in your situation, in your involvements, and in your relationships. You aren't burdened with guilt and worries—nor do you allow situations and circumstances to take the peace out of your heart. You know the "Prince of Peace." His presence stills your inner being. Faith in Him and His promises creates a peace "that passes all human understanding."

College student Mel Lehman says in *Christian Living:*

> For any man caught up with a cause, particularly in such an obviously righteous one as the peace movement, the temptation is great to place one's claim for righteousness in what he believes and preaches, rather than in the authenticity of his daily relationship with God, man and himself.

I read a motto recently that said, "Only in obedience is there peace." This includes:

> Obedience to God and His Word.
> Obedience to law and those persons in authority —in the community, church, and nation.
> Obedience to limits and guidelines necessary for happy family relationships.
> Obedience to rules at your place of work—office, school, hospital, etc.
> Obedience to rules of your profession.
> Obedience to the moral code.

The parent is a peacemaker in the home. Sometimes that means being a referee at the children's games or quarrels. At other times it's giving an idea to resolve an argument or conflict you're involved in. You work through conflicts. You choose ways to avoid problems and conflicts. You don't call attention to someone's actions or characteristics just to embarrass or irritate him.

The peacemaker mother checks her words and controls her tongue. To criticize, or to complain about a leaky faucet or a broken knob immediately when hubby comes into the house at the end of the day, doesn't make for peace.

The Bible says, "If possible, so far as it depends upon you, live peaceably with all" (Romans 12:18).

Soft words drive away strife. Remember, it takes two to quarrel, so don't add fuel to a smoldering fire.

A peacemaker freely compliments, expresses a word of appreciation, or is just cheerful. Sometimes it's just being quiet. It's using common sense in your home and in the marriage relationship. If you are blamed wrongly, state your feelings and don't attack the person, or condemn and judge.

You avoid conflict with the children when possible. You try to go to the root of the conflict. You deal with causes rather than effects.

A peacemaker sometimes has to separate quarreling, angry children. She will teach them to take turns. She'll never be a peacemaker if she herself gets angry and says cruel, unkind words, or forces the child into quietness through brutal treatment. Sometimes peacemaking means taking time to play with the children, or to introduce new and interesting games, crafts, or hobbies. Or perhaps it's just being ready to listen.

You introduce a positive solution to the children's quarrels with their playmates. One mother noticed that her son's vaulting pole was the envy of the neighbor boys. She related this to her husband, who then gathered the boys together, went into the woods, and made poles for every boy.

Someone has said, "Peace begins in our nurseries." Mothers, you hold the key to a peaceful world. Beginning in those early, impressionable years and through all the different ages and stages when you show love, gentleness, goodness, kindness, and forgiveness, with firm but loving discipline and guidelines, you are sowing the seeds of peace.

By example and careful teaching, you show the way of love and peace. You try to avoid triggering arguments. You speak softly to end quarrels. You help children learn how to live with each other.

You are a peacemaker when you are the first one to admit a misunderstanding, angry or unkind words, and then ask forgiveness of your husband or of your child. You will be interested in promoting peace outside the home, in the neighborhood. You'll encourage your children to accept and relate to the child who's ignored, to invite him over to play, to befriend him at school. You show how to overcome evil with good.

On a high-school campus, in a frantic desire to be accepted, a boy became a deceitful braggart. The other boys decided they were going to put him in his place and beat him up. A classmate, Ralph, told his father about this. The understanding father said, "Son, the boy is lonely. None of you have accepted him, have you? Why don't you go back to school and show him some kindness."

Ralph prayed to God for wisdom.

Several days later he came home and reported, "I told the boys what you said, Dad. We decided you were right. I'm helping him to learn how to play tennis. The other boys are relating to him, too. He's different. He isn't trying to pick a fight anymore. He's really nice, Dad."

I personally am grateful for our president's attempts to make peace. I appreciate individuals and groups who have taken a positive, peaceful approach in stating their wishes for peace to the proper authorities.

But what can you do? Doctor Alfred A. Weinstein says in *Good Business:*

> You may think there is not much that any one person can do toward achieving world peace. Yet, if every person who believed in the ideas in the Golden Rule, the Sermon on the Mount, and the Ten Commandments would begin practicing them in his own sphere, the combined effect would be world-shaking.

You can have faith in God who is the God of today—as well as of history. You can pray for peace.

Doctor Walter McCluhen, the noted Canadian authority on communications, says prayer is the greatest and most radical force available. It breaks down structures which man alone is unable to break. It penetrates areas man can't enter.

Recently, I heard a speaker say that the truly radical Christian is a praying Christian. If you want to be a radical peacemaker, start here. Pray for peace, first in your own life, in your own sphere of action. Then pray for peace in your relationships with others—your husband, children, parents, in-laws, neighbors, employees, or employer. Pray for peace in the community, state, nation, and world.

When you pray sincerely and frequently, you will get involved as you respond to the nudging of the Spirit—but your actions will be peaceable, for the fruit of the Spirit is peace.

> The wisdom that comes from God is first utterly pure, then peace-loving, gentle, approachable, full of

tolerant thoughts and kindly actions, with no breath
of favoritism or hint of hypocrisy. And the wise are
peacemakers who go on quietly sowing for a harvest
of righteousness—in other people and in themselves.

James 3:17, 18

"Blessed are the peacemakers." They are happy because they make others happy. They are happy because
they aren't worrying—nor are they tense and uptight.
They don't have to solve the problems. They are a part
of the solution.

Lord, make me an instrument of Thy peace.
Where there is hate, may I bring love;
Where offense, may I bring pardon;
May I bring union in place of discord;
Truth, replacing error;
Faith, where once there was doubt;
Hope, for despair;
Light, where was darkness;
Joy to replace sadness.
Make me not to so crave to be loved as to love.
Help me to learn that in giving I may receive;
In forgetting self, I may find life eternal.

SAINT FRANCIS OF ASSISI

30
The Giver of Peace

Throughout these chapters I've frequently referred to
Jesus—the Source of peace with self and with others.
"Prince of Peace" is His name.

I believe with all my heart that He is the Giver of peace. At the same time, we have a responsible position to act out this peace—and that is what these chapters are all about.

I focus also on another key word—*faith.* I must stress it. I feel compelled to.

We must bring Jesus—peace, love, joy—to this old world now, in this generation! It's a special privilege for parents and adults who know and love Him. He is the only way to peace. However, faith is the means by which we reach Him—faith in God and His words.

Evangelist Billy Graham's wife, Ruth, was quoted in *Decision* magazine as having said:

> In a world of confusion and uncertainties I will give them [my children] the eternal verities of the Word of God. In a world that has lost its moorings, I will try to help them cast their anchor while they are young, on the goodness and mercy of God. In a scientific age, I will teach them the importance of faith. In a day of shifting morals, I will teach them the unchanging absolutes of the Ten Commandments. At a time when aimlessness has become a way of life, I will teach them that man's chief end is still "to glorify God and to enjoy Him forever.

Our children are caught in an age of confusion and uncertainties. Parents and teachers are confused as to methods of discipline. Permissiveness has been taught as the way of love and understanding. Now authorities say to use control. Firm discipline shows love!

Furthermore, too many children are shuttled back and forth weekly between two sets of parents, two separate homes, two distinct forms of thought and life. They're torn apart between two loves.

Wars and tragedies loom large in their minds. A niece of mine reported her problems as a teacher of children whose fathers experienced war in Vietnam.

In one of our local schools, several children attended for only two weeks. Then they were gone. The family, as is one out of five, was again on the move.

Furthermore, the world has lost its moorings. We're living in an age of shifting morals. It seems right is wrong and wrong is right. Self—its personal desires and its passions—is the guide for many! They have no real aim in life.

Man does what he pleases. He hates, so he kills. He wants another man's wife, so he gets her. He wants to satisfy his passions, so he laughs at self-control. He wants to disobey parents, so he defies them. He wants to "do his own thing," so he rejects all authority—even God! He wants to work on the Lord's day, so he doesn't keep it as a day of rest and worship. He substitutes other "gods" and worships them.

People sell their souls for pleasure, for fame, for fortune. Competition, pressures, and false values dictate people's ideas and goals. They vainly search for happiness, unaware that happiness cannot be found in an aimless, self-gratifying existence. Happiness is a by-product of a life of love and concern for others.

Faith accepts God as demonstrated through Jesus Christ's life. He left His heavenly home with its perfection—perfect love and joy, no hate, no sickness, no selfishness. He abandoned it all to bring love, joy, and peace to the individual heart, to make you a whole person in a broken world.

He taught the moral law and even more. He taught that law is not necessarily confined to action. It begins in the thought life, in attitudes and motives. He came to give you the courage and power to think and live rightly.

In this scientific age, your child needs faith. Faith is

believing. It's accepting that which cannot be seen and which cannot be proven by equations. You believe because God says so. You've experienced God's truths in your life.

During a serious illness, healing came, surprising all doctors and friends. You know why—God promised it.

When you were alone, He was your companion. When you were in financial difficulties, He helped you through. When you were faced with an important decision, He led in unplanned ways. Faith is real to you.

Even in an atomic age, your faith brings peace. You join the psalmist, who says that God is his refuge—a rock, eternal and unmovable; God is his strength, so he isn't afraid even though kingdoms fall, even though the earth is destroyed, even though the mountains get moved into the middle of the ocean (*see* Psalm 46).

Through your faith, your child learns about God.

You may educate your child in the best schools—from the nursery on through college.

You may dress him in the latest fashions.

You may make available for him the best of medical care.

You may teach him all the social graces.

You may provide music lessions, and he may become an accomplished musician.

But these are not enough, as good and important as they are! Supplying these without guiding your child to find Jesus, the Prince of Peace, is stopping short of your parental responsibility.

Education passes away.
Culture changes.
Fashions disappear.
Wealth vanishes.
Health fails

> But faith in God lasts on,
> And on, and on.
> When all else is gone,
> God is still there.

Faith is a gift from God. It comes from reading His Word and from an intimate acquaintance with Him. You don't need cash or a credit account! It's an exchange gift. You give yourself to God, then He gives Himself to you. You harmonize your thoughts with His. You believe His words. You obey them. And what is the result of faith? Peace!

Now your compelling passion is to help others find Jesus, the Prince of Peace, who is the answer to this world's ills. You realize that a nation can be changed only by individuals. A concept, an idea, must be embodied in a person.

When peace is wrapped up in a human heart and in daily words and actions; when there's peace with self, with God, and with neighbors, there will be peace in this world.

In your heart, is there faith? Have you found the Giver of peace?

31
Words of Peace
From the Holy Scriptures

Thé LORD will give strength unto his people; the LORD will bless his people with peace.

Psalm 29:11 KJV

And the work of righteousness shall be peace; and the effect of righteousness [is] quietness and assurance for ever.

And my people shall dwell in a peaceable habitation, and in sure dwellings, and in quiet resting places;

[Even] When it shall hail, coming down on the forest; and the city shall be low in a low place.

Isaiah 32:17–19 KJV

For unto us a child is born . . . and his name shall be called Wonderful, Counseller, The mighty God, The everlasting Father, The Prince of Peace.

Isaiah 9:6 KJV

For unto you is born this day . . . a Saviour, which is Christ the Lord. . . . Glory to God in the highest, and on earth peace, good will toward men.

Luke 2:11,14 KJV

Because of and through the heart of tender mercy and loving kindness of our God, a Light from on high will dawn upon us and visit [us], To shine upon and give light to those who sit in darkness and in the shadow of death, to direct and guide our feet in a straight line into [the] way of peace.

Luke 1:78,79 AMPLIFIED

He that would love life,
And see good days,
Let him refrain his tongue from evil,
And his lips that they speak no guile:
And let him turn away from evil, and do good;
Let him seek peace and pursue it.

1 Peter 3:10,11